WARRIOR • 126

HIGHLANDER IN THE FRENCH-INDIAN WAR

1756–67

IAN MACPHERSON McCULLOCH   ILLUSTRATED BY STEVE NOON

First published in Great Britain in 2008 by Osprey Publishing,
Midland House, West Way, Botley, Oxford OX2 0PH, UK
443 Park Avenue South, New York, NY 10016, USA
E-mail: info@ospreypublishing.com

A CIP catalog record for this book is available from the British Library

ISBN: 978 1 84603 274 5

Page layout by: Scribe, Oxford, UK
Index by Alison Worthington
Typeset in Sabon and Myriad Pro
Originated by PDQ Digital Media Solutions
Printed in China through Worldprint Ltd

08 09 10 11 12   10 9 8 7 6 5 4 3 2 1

FOR A CATALOG OF ALL BOOKS PUBLISHED BY OSPREY MILITARY AND
AVIATION PLEASE CONTACT:

NORTH AMERICA
Osprey Direct, c/o Random House Distribution Center, 400 Hahn Road,
Westminster, MD 21157
E-mail: info@ospreydirect.com

ALL OTHER REGIONS
Osprey Direct UK, P.O. Box 140 Wellingborough, Northants, NN8 2FA, UK
E-mail: info@ospreydirect.co.uk

Osprey Publishing is supporting the Woodland Trust, the UK's leading
woodland conservation charity, by funding the dedication of trees.

www.ospreypublishing.com

ARTIST'S NOTE

Readers may care to note that the original paintings from which the
color plates in this book were prepared are available for private sale.
All reproduction copyright whatsoever is retained by the Publishers.
All inquiries should be addressed to:

Steve Noon
50 Colchester Avenue
Penylan
Cardiff
CF23 9BP

The Publishers regret that they can enter into no correspondence upon
this matter.

ACKNOWLEDGEMENTS

The author wishes to thank, first and foremost, Steve Noon, the artist, who
brought this subject to life. Thanks also go out to the many people and
institutions in Canada, the United States and United Kingdom that assisted
in the preparation of this book, with special thanks to: Bob Erlandson;
Kenneth Stiles; Tim Todish; Cathy & Jerry Seymour of Paramount Press;
Robert "Griff" Griffing; Robert Andrews; Dr John Houlding; Dr Bill Forbes;
Dr Stephen Brumwell; Cluny – Sir William Allan Macpherson; Dave Miller
of the Bushy Run Battlefield site; Tommy Smyth, Black Watch Archivist,
Balhousie Castle; LtCol Bruce Bolton, former commanding officer,
The Black Watch (Royal Highland Regiment) of Canada and former
executive director, David M. Stewart; Black Watch (RHR) Museum
of Canada; Chris Fox of the Fort Ticonderoga Museum; the National
Archives of Canada; and the Library of Congress.

Finally, an old chestnut bears repetition. Despite the impressive array
of talented and knowledgeable folks listed above, any errors or omissions
in the book are entirely the author's responsibility.

AUTHOR'S NOTE TO THE SOURCES

The many eye-witness accounts that have been sourced to tell James
Thompson of Inverness' tale, including his own, come from myriad sources:
the official reports and returns from the War Office; the succession and
commission books; surviving orderly books such as those of James Stewart
of Urrard, 42nd Foot, kept from 1759 to 1761 or Captain John Nairn's 1762
Orderly Book for the 78th at Quebec; Gaelic songs and poems composed
before, during and after several of the battles; and British and North
American newspapers and magazines of the day. On a more personal level,
I have used published and unpublished memoirs and journals of Highland
officers, NCOs, and, in one rare case, a private soldier, many of which
appear in the select bibliography at the back. Numerous letters sent home
by officers and men to relatives have also survived and many of these
found their way into print at the time, or were printed later in family
histories. Many bundles of letters have also been coaxed out of the relative
obscurity of various private family collections and collated for public
consumption in various national repositories such as the National Archives
of Scotland, the National Archives of Canada, the National Archives in
London and the Library of Congress in Washington, DC.

CONTENTS

HIGHLANDER IN THE FRENCH-INDIAN WAR

INTRODUCTION

No great mischief if they fall.
– Major James Wolfe

The Seven Years' War (1755–63) was the world's first global war, a conflict spanning the continents of North America, Europe, and Asia. Fought principally between Britain, France, and their respective allies, it became known more colloquially in American history books as the French & Indian War (or French-Indian War). It was Anglo-French rivalries in the teeming forests and rich river plains of the disputed Ohio River valley that led to a fateful exchange of shots between Virginian provincials and British regulars led by a young officer named George Washington and a force of French soldiers and their Indian allies. The result was a diplomatic incident that escalated into a crisis between Britain and France, both dispatching regular troops to North America in anticipation of hostilities.

Before war was even officially declared in April 1755, MajGen Edward Braddock advanced with 2,200 British regulars and American provincials against Fort Duquesne, a wooden French fort on the Forks of the Ohio River and site of the present-day city of Pittsburgh in western Pennsylvania. One of three British expeditions against French frontier posts, Braddock's force was surprised 7 miles short of its objective by a vastly inferior force of Indians and French colonial soldiers using Indian tactics of envelopment and concealment. Braddock was killed and his force dispersed.

The 2nd Division of the 42nd Foot parade in review on Glasgow Green in April 1756, prior to their departure for North America. On the left, Major Duncan Campbell of Inverawe, attended by drummers relaying his orders, puts the half-companies through their firings of blank ammunition for the benefit of the inspecting officers, while spectators look on with interest. (Trustees of the Black Watch Museum)

The shocking news of the "massacre" on the Monongahela River reached the Scottish Highlands in late 1755. It stoked an already busy rumor-mill that new Highland battalions (based on the model of the 42nd Foot) would soon be authorized and raised to go overseas to North America with Lord Loudon, the newly appointed commander-in-chief for America, in 1756.

Initially, resistance to such a scheme was predictable and emanated straight from the top. Neither the British king, George II, nor his son, the Duke of Cumberland, could countenance the addition of any more Highland regiments to the army's establishment – the unpleasant memories of Culloden and the 1745 Uprising under Bonnie Prince Charlie just a decade earlier were still fresh in their minds. The Duke of Argyll, (or the "governor" of Scotland as the Duke of Newcastle styled him), was the principal lobbyist for the creation of new Highland battalions. Argyll had astutely bided his time, realizing that the foreign policy direction taken in December 1756 by the recently installed Secretary of State, William Pitt the Elder (1708–78), would soon support rather than hinder his proposals, as Pitt's policies called for the vigorous acquisition and defense of colonies. The Duke of Cumberland, not noted for his quick-wittedness, was bright enough to realize that if he did not readily acquiesce to the raising of at least a few new Highland regiments, he might lose some of his beloved "Flanderkin" regiments to the North American theater. He quietly withdrew his objections. Orders and warrants for two new Highland battalions for service in North America were quickly issued.

Six years before the outbreak of the Seven Years' War, a young, pragmatic British Army officer stationed in the Highlands, who had witnessed the ferocity of the last Highland charge on British soil at Culloden in 1746, was of the opinion that Highlanders would make excellent irregulars to combat the Indians in the wilds of North America. Major James Wolfe therefore wrote to a friend in 1750: "I should imagine that two or three independent Highland companies might be of use. They are hardy, intrepid, accustomed to a rough country, and no great mischief if they fall."

It was certainly not a new idea to use Highland troops for overseas service in America, though Wolfe and William Pitt are sometimes touted as having been the propagators of such a plan. In 1740 Gen James Oglethorpe, colonel of the 42nd Regiment of Foot stationed in the fledgling colony of Georgia, had raised on his own initiative the first fully plaided Scottish unit of the British regular army in North America. This Highland company fought on several occasions against the Spaniards in eastern Florida and was finally disbanded on December 24, 1746. Ironically, Oglethorpe's 42nd Foot in Georgia would yield its famous number "42" to the Black Watch.

Who, then, were the Highlanders of the Seven Years' War who would forge such an enviable reputation for unshakable loyalty and courage in North America, a reputation that would ensure them a permanent place on the establishment of the British Army for centuries to come? Where did they come from; what were their beliefs and culture; did they come willingly; did they ever get homesick; what were their expectations, and how were they perceived? Owing to the Highlanders' oral culture and the Gaelic language, no one has ever seriously examined the Highlanders' personal experiences in North America. Much of the following narrative has been gleaned from letters, diaries, memoirs, and eye-witness accounts of the Highlanders who actually soldiered in North America, as well as from their translated Gaelic poetry and songs composed during the period. This is their story.

Major General David Stewart of Garth (1772–1829), a former Black Watch officer and a staunch advocate of Highland dress, did more than anyone else to create the modern image of the Highlander in the 19th century. His *Sketches of the Character, Manners and Present State of the Highlanders of Scotland*, first published in 1822, has underpinned every subsequent account of the Highlands and their regiments to this day. (Private collection)

While serving in the Highlands of Scotland post-Culloden, a very young James Wolfe confessed to a friend in Nova Scotia that the Highland rebels he pursued would make excellent irregulars to combat the Indians in the wilds of North America. At Louisburg in 1758, Fraser's Highlanders nicknamed Wolfe "The Red-Haired Corporal," an allusion to his familiarity and the gold aiguillette (similar to a corporal's white worsted shoulder knot) that hung from his right shoulder. (National Archives of Canada)

CHRONOLOGY

1755

July   Massacre of Braddock's British-American expedition sent to take Fort Duquesne (Pittsburgh) from the French on the Forks of the Ohio.

1756

January   The 42nd Foot (Black Watch) ordered to North America. Recruiting parties sent to Highlands for an additional 600 recruits.

April   The 1st Division of the 42nd Foot sails for North America.

June   The 2nd Division of the 42nd Foot follows.

1757

January   The 1st (Montgomery's) and 2nd (Fraser's) Highland Battalions ordered to be raised.

July   Montgomery's Highlanders (initially numbered the 62nd Foot, then renumbered 77th Foot), set sail for Charles Town, SC. Fraser's Highlanders (initially numbered 63rd Foot, renumbered 78th) set sail for Halifax, NS.

August   Lord Loudon's expedition from Halifax to Louisburg canceled. The 42nd Foot returns to New York for the winter. The 78th Foot arrives at Halifax and temporarily garrisons Dartmouth.

September   The 77th Foot lands in Charles Town, SC, and go into garrison.

October   The 78th Foot is ordered from Dartmouth, NS, to winter quarters in Connecticut.

1758

April   The 77th Foot is ordered to Pennsylvania to take part in Gen John

Arriving in transports, this is the view of New York that all three Highland regiments would have first experienced as they staged through on their many campaigns. Seen here, the Union Jack flies over Fort George on the southern tip of Manhattan Island, garrisoned by soldiers of the Black Watch during the winter of 1757/58. (Library of Congress)

Forbes' expedition against Fort Duquesne. The 78th Foot is sent to Halifax from Connecticut to join MajGen Jeffery Amherst's expedition against Louisburg.

June   The 78th Foot lands in the first wave at Kennington Cove near Louisburg, June 8, and participates in the siege of Louisburg.

July   Battle of Ticonderoga, July 8. Louisburg on Cape Breton Island capitulates to Amherst's army, July 26. A second battalion of the 42nd Foot is ordered raised in Scotland for service in North America, and the regiment is officially awarded the title The Royal Highland Regiment by the king.

August   The 77th Foot reaches Fort Bedford in western Pennsylvania. Numerous detachments assigned to building Forbes Road.

September Major James Grant's force of 77th Foot, Royal American, and provincial detachments, is routed in a failed raid on Fort Duquesne from Fort Ligonier. General Amherst and five regiments, including the 78th, land at Boston and march overland to Abercromby's assistance in New York colony.

October   The 78th is ordered into winter quarters at Schenectady, NY, and garrisons the newly built Fort Stanwix for the winter.

November The French blow up and abandon Fort Duquesne on the approach of Forbes' army in western Pennsylvania.

1759

April   The 77th Foot (less two companies) is ordered north from Carlisle, PA, to Albany, NY, to join Amherst's expedition against Montréal.

July–Aug The 1st/42nd Foot and 77th Foot participate in Amherst's capture of Fort Ticonderoga and Crown Point. The 2nd /42nd Foot arrives at Albany and marches to Oswego on Lake Ontario.

September The 78th Foot fights at the Plains of Abraham on September 13 under Gen James Wolfe and garrisons Québec for the winter.

A reconstructed bird's-eye view by Charles Stotz of what the British Fort Ligonier, situated about 50 miles southeast of Pittsburgh, looked like in 1758–59. The fort was built overlooking the Loyalhanna or Loyalhannon Creek by Highlanders, other regulars, and provincial soldiers and was named for Field Marshal John Ligonier. (Historical Society of Western Pennsylvania, Pittsburgh)

Robert Griffing's painting entitled *Warriors* shows a private soldier of the 77th conferring with an Indian ally before Grant's disastrous march against Fort Duquesne in September 1758. The affinity and respect between the Highlanders and Indian warriors was noted by numerous observers. Just two years later, the Highlanders and Cherokee would be enemies. (Robert Griffing & Paramount Press)

1760

April	The 78th Foot fights at the Battle of Sillery (Sainte Foy), Québec, April 28.
May	Six companies of both the 77th Foot and Royal Scots are dispatched from Albany to the Carolinas to fight Cherokees. The siege of Québec by Gén Levis' Franco-Canadian army is broken.
June/Aug	Both battalions of the 42nd and the 77th Foot (eight companies) march to Oswego for Amherst's invasion of Canada by way of Lake Ontario and down the St Lawrence River. The 77th Foot and Royal Scots burn the Cherokee Lower Towns and fight at the Battle of Etchoe Pass.
September	Amherst's, Murray's, and Haviland's armies converge on Montréal and New France capitulates, September 8. The 1st and 2nd Battalions of the Royal Highlanders garrison Montréal for the winter. The 78th Foot is sent downriver to Québec City and its dependencies to do garrison duty until the end of the war.
October	Eight companies of the 77th sent to garrison Halifax, NS, for the winter. Six Carolina companies of the 77th arrive at Albany and are also ordered to NS.

1761

April Nine companies of the 77th Foot are dispatched for service in the Caribbean.

Sept/Oct The 1st and 2nd /42nd Foot prepare for the Caribbean campaign against Martinique.

1762

February The 42nd and 77th Foot (as part of MajGen Robert Monckton's army) capture Martinique.

June The 42nd and 77th Foot land in Cuba to participate in the siege of Havana.

August Havana surrenders. Remnants of the fever-ridden battalions of the 42nd and the 77th Foot are sent back to Long Island, NY, to recuperate.

1763

February Treaty of Paris ends Seven Years' War.

May Western Indians under Pontiac attack British forts.

June/July Remnants of the 42nd and 77th Foot form Col Henri Bouquet's relief expedition to Fort Pitt and march to Ligonier.

August Composite battalion of 42nd and 77th Highlanders fight at Battle of Bushy Run, August 5–6. Fort Pitt is relieved, August 9.

December The 77th and 78th Foot are officially disbanded and officers placed on half-pay. Many Highlanders transfer to other regiments, while others are discharged to return home to Scotland. Some elect to stay and settle in colonies.

1764

July Col Bouquet's punitive expedition against the Ohio Valley Indians, comprising six companies of Royal Highlanders, two companies of Royal Americans and some provincials, departs Fort Pitt.

November The western Indians submit at Muskingum. The 42nd Foot returns to garrison Fort Pitt for the winter.

1765

Aug/Sept A force of 42nd soldiers descends the Ohio from Fort Pitt to take possession of the Illinois territories.

October Highlanders take possession of Fort de Chartres near present-day St Louis. Three companies of the 42nd are left to garrison Fort Pitt for winter. The remainder return to garrison Philadelphia.

Captain Charles Macdonell's composite light infantry company, comprising Highlanders of the 42nd, 77th, and 78th Regiments of Foot, storms Signal Hill, Newfoundland, at dawn on September 15, 1762. The attack successfully routed three French grenadier companies and ensured the eventual recapture of the town and harbor for British forces. (Painting by Steve Noon from Osprey's Warrior 88: *British Light Infantryman of the Seven Years' War* by Ian McCulloch and Tim Todish)

Detail from a 1764 map cartouche depicting Col Henri Bouquet's conference with the Muskingum Indians of the Ohio country. The Highlander on the left is the only known contemporary image of a 42nd soldier serving in North America during the French-Indian War. As the soldier is on guard duty, he is dressed in full plaids instead of his normal campaign dress of "little kilt" or philabeg. (Library of Congress)

1767

June   The 42nd Highlanders relieved by 18th Foot, and sail home from New York.

July   Remnants of Black Watch arrive in Cork, Ireland.

RECRUITMENT AND ENLISTMENT

Recruit the Highland Lads
– From a recruitment publication, "The New Song"

The 42nd Foot was the first Highland regiment sent to North America during the French-Indian War. When the beating orders first arrived in Ireland in January 1756, the regiment was dispersed in garrison towns and woefully under strength. Orders authorized the commanding officer, Francis Grant, to recruit up to a wartime strength of 1,000 sentinels. He immediately sent the majority of his junior officers, non-commissioned officers (NCOs) and pipers across to Scotland under the command of the regimental second-in-command, Duncan Campbell of Inverawe, to start recruiting the additional 600 private men urgently needed. Once these new companies were fully recruited, dressed, equipped, and given some rudimentary training, they would constitute the 2nd Division and follow on to America after the 1st Division.

Posters and printed notices appeared on tavern walls and in public places throughout Scotland, including this broadside entitled "A New Song" which was published in Edinburgh, claiming:

> Lord Loudoun sent to our gracious King
> Desiring of His Majesty
> For to recruit the Highland Lads
> And send them over to North-America
>
> ...Recruit me none but the old Clans,
> Camel's [Campbells], Mackenzy's, Fraser's and Grant's
> For they are brought up to the Sword,
> Such warlike men Lord Loudoun wants.

This "New Song" would not have made sense to most potential 42nd recruits, as they did not speak the King's English. No doubt the pamphlet had a Gaelic counterpart, as the song's message and awkward phrasing strongly indicate it to be a loose translation from the original Gaelic. It was cunningly crafted to appeal to most Highlanders of the day with its call to "the old Clans" and its traditional bardic emphasis on the honor to be accrued in "going for a soldier."

The promise of using Highland weapons on the king's enemies was certainly irresistible to some, as the Highland clans were still forbidden to wear the *feileadh mór* (full plaids, or literally, the "big wrap") or to carry arms under the Proscription Act put in place after the 1745 Uprising. Only in the king's service would they be able to don "Bonnets blue, with Sword and pistol and warlike Goods," and "chace the Indians thro' the Woods."

Recruiting was a task easily accomplished and many recruits were impressed from a veritable pool of landless and unemployed laborers. Agriculture was limited in the north of Britain, and to make matters worse, the crops had failed two years in a row and famine ravaged the Highlands. The 2nd Division, after their review at Glasgow in April 1756, spent another two months training and left Glasgow on June 7, 1756, for Greenock, where they embarked the following day. The embarkation return signed by Major Duncan Campbell shows 646 all ranks bound for North America. Aboard were one major, two captains, six lieutenants, nine ensigns, one chaplain, 17 sergeants, two drummers, ten additional drummers (untrained), and 576 recruits. The 42nd Foot, commanded by LtCol Grant and comprising five companies of 100, was still at sea and approaching New York, having left Plymouth on April 15, two months earlier.

Both divisions of the 42nd Foot arrived too late in America for any serious campaigning and the reunited regiment found itself assigned to winter quarters along the Mohawk River in upstate New York. The bulk of the Highlanders were stationed at Schenectady, and as they celebrated their first Hogmanay in the New World, beating orders were issued for two new additional Highland battalions to be raised in Scotland for service in North America.

On January 4, 1757, Lord Barrington, the Secretary of War responsible for the raising and manning of regiments for the army, contacted Archibald Montgomery, brother of the 10th Earl of Eglinton, and Simon Fraser, whose father Lord Lovat had been executed for treason for his part in the 1745 Uprising. Montgomery and Fraser were instructed to "Raise a Highland Battalion of Foot, under your command, which is to Consist of Ten Companies of Four Serjeants, Four Corporals, Two Drummers, and One Hundred Effective Private Men in each Company, besides Commission Officers…"

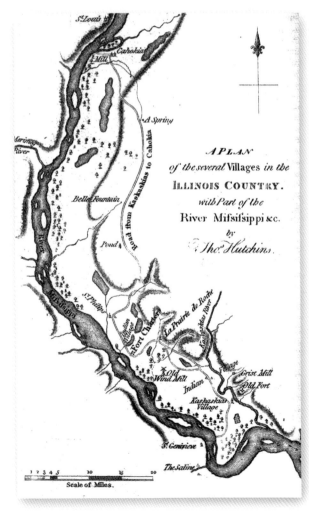

In 1765, 100 Highlanders under the command of Capt Thomas Stirling traveled by boats down the Ohio River to take possession of Fort de Chartres on the Mississippi River near present-day St Louis. This map appeared in *A History of the Late War* written by a 77th Foot officer, Lt Thomas Mante, and shows the locations of the principal French and Indian villages in the region taken over by the British. (Private collection)

After the devastating blow of Culloden in 1746, all Highlanders were forbidden by law to carry arms or wear the kilt like the fiercely independent clansman depicted in this painting by Robert Griffing. The only exception was those willing to don the redcoat in the service of the British king. For this reason, as well as economic factors, many former Jacobites flocked to join the new Highland regiments raised for service in North America. (Robert Griffing & Paramount Press)

Their commissions made them lieutenant colonels, commandants of the 1st and 2nd Highland Battalions respectively, confirmed by Royal Warrant on "the 5th Day of January 1757 in the 30th Year of our Reign." These new units, originally designated the 1st and 2nd Highland Battalions, were initially numbered the 62nd and 63rd Regiments of Foot, but were subsequently renumbered the 77th (Montgomery's) and 78th (Fraser's) the following year when several older established regiments of the British Army had their second battalions turned into new stand-alone regiments.

The majority of recruits enlisted for these new Highland regiments spoke little or no English, so Argyll, writing to the Duke of Atholl in 1757, insisted that all officers forwarded for potential company commands in Fraser's and Montgomery's Highlanders must speak Erse, the prevailing term in the 18th century for the Gaelic or "Irish" language. More importantly, there was the immediate requirement to train and discipline the raw recruits. Thus the rapid selection of the NCOs, who would form the backbone of both battalions and ensure that the new units would meet minimum standards as "British" regiments, was even more critical to the success of the experiment.

Here Lord Barrington himself intervened to ensure the new Highland regiments got off on the right footing. On January 25, 1757, he wrote to the senior officer commanding the Foot Guards, directing that 25 men who were ready to be sergeants were to be drafted from his regiment, recommending those "who can speak the Highland language, Ten of whom are to be turned over to Lieut Colo Montgomery's battalion and the remaining Fifteen to Lieut Colo Fraser's Battalion." The same letter went out to eight other regiments (a good indication of how prevalent Highlanders serving in the regular British line regiments had become by the mid-18th century), directing each to provide a certain quota of "Highland-speaking NCOs" to the new Highland battalions for a total of 105 NCOs.

When these Highland battalions reached North America, other Highland NCOs and officers eager to serve with their own countrymen would request transfers from other line regiments already serving in the region. For example, Sgt Donald Macleod, 42nd Foot, transferred to the 78th Foot, being a swordsman of some repute and an experienced drill sergeant. Sergeant Lauchlin McPherson, with the 40th Foot in Nova Scotia, petitioned Lord Loudoun for a transfer to either one of the new Highland battalions bound for North America, convinced that "some of his Friends and neighbours must be among them" and offered to take a reduction in rank to private for the privilege.

One of the most interesting personal accounts of a Highlander who soldiered in North America during the Seven Years' War is found in an old accounting ledger in the possession of the National Archives of Canada. There, on the blank reverse pages scrawled in pencil, are the stories and colorful anecdotes of Grenadier Sgt James Thompson who served in the 78th Foot.

An astute observer with an eye for a humorous story or yarn, the young sergeant by the war's end was a veteran of Louisburg 1758, the Plains of Abraham 1759, and the little-known Battle of Sillery outside Québec City in 1760. Thompson, in effect, was one of the unofficial bards of his regiment and his stories bring to life the frontline experiences of the Highland soldier as seen from the battle and siege lines, as well as from the daily routine of camp or garrison life. Of particular interest are his descriptions of encounters with Indians, his friends in the ranks, his officers, fellow freemasons, and the Canadian inhabitants and American families that he subsequently came to know.

As the 78th Foot was being raised, Thompson, a native of Inverness, had nurtured aspirations of being a junior officer. The grenadier company commander of the 78th, Charles Baillie, was his best friend, but this connection was not enough to secure him one of the scarce commissions eagerly sought after by the disenfranchised Jacobite gentry of the Highlands. Many of the latter were hoping that service in the Georgian king's army would restore their good name and help in recovering their estates,

A reconstruction of a 42nd field officer c.1756 by Clyde A. Risley. The deep scarlet of the officer's jacket, his wide lapels, the engraved gorget worn around the neck, the gold trim or lace around his button holes and cuffs, as well as the well-crafted sword on his hip, were all indicators of his officer's status and he could be readily identified as such at a distance by a private soldier. (Private collection)

confiscated as punishment for their participation on the losing side of the 1745 Uprising. Thompson thus volunteered as a soldier, but on the understanding that his friend would actively recommend him for the first vacant ensigncy when it became available and, until that time, would serve as a sergeant in the grenadier company. Unfortunately, Thompson's mentor and protector was one of the first killed at the Louisburg landings in 1758, and all hopes of preferment died with Baillie.

To understand the recruiting of Thompson's regiment, we can follow the efforts of his unit's senior major, James Clephane, who would meet his assigned quota of recruits by hiring John Strachen, a professional recruiter. Clephane's relatives and network of friends would also become involved. His most ardent supporter was his sister Betty, wife of Hugh Rose of Kilravock. She actively recruited as far away as Perthshire and Angus with the assistance of several women around Nairnshire, and fretted that the 77th Foot recruiting parties were outstripping the Fraser Highlanders in obtaining the best men. In one of Betty Rose's letters to her brother in London, she voiced sympathy for the difficulties facing Col Fraser:

> ...I think [he] has got the most difficult [task] to act, for Montgomery's people is just planted round them, for except Mr. Baillie in Rosshire, and Mr. Rose in Murray [Moray]; I see no other help that poor Fraser has got... Colonel Fraser is in want of some proper people about him; I was this day up very early giveing him a motherly breakfast and setting him off about his business.

The "motherly" Mrs Rose soon had a "very numbrous band" of recruits for her brother's company, but demurred in forwarding them on to Inverness, preferring to keep the young men nearby on the estate so that she could make sure "their Bellys may be well-filled, and if thay be, thay will cast a dash, for thay are realy hansome Boys." Betty Rose quickly established a reputation for paying top bounty money for recruits, much to the dismay of her thrifty husband. The result was that many of the best Highlanders flocked to her door, cognizant that their landlords from the surrounding district would soon probably force them to enlist anyway and that they might as well offer their services to Major Clephane's sister. Mrs Rose could proudly boast that all her brother's recruits were "tip-top fellows" and "Sterling volenteers," in contrast to those raised by the local "Grandees" who had rousted "out their people as if they had their press act in force for it."

An attestation roll of the Dundee men in Major Clephane's company gives us a glimpse into the social background of some 78th recruits, the average age of the group being 18.4 years of age. The majority of the new recruits listed were either laborers or weavers, deflating the popular myth and stereotype that has been perpetuated by Stewart of Garth – viz. all Highlanders were warriors from birth with a natural talent for war. In truth, the major part of a clan's manpower was devoted to the land, eking out a meager subsistence on the poor Highland soil, tending their black cattle, fishing, or collecting dulse. In 1757, the young recruits had at most been only seven or eight years of age when older brothers, fathers, and grandfathers had willingly (or unwillingly) fought at Culloden, if they had fought at all. None of the teenage laborers, cottars, or weavers stepping forward to serve in James Clephane's company could be characterized as "professional warriors," most having never wielded anything more dangerous than a plough or scythe.

Impressments were common in the raising of both new Highland battalions. A recent act of Parliament had given local magistrates the necessary power to impress all unemployed men by special decree, causing Lady Ballindalloch to confess that her brother-in-law, Major James, had probably not recruited such large numbers in such a short time for the 77th without "takeing some men from their poor wives and children. I daresay there is not many spared out of Inveraven." Many unemployed men with the threat of impressments looming opted for the lesser of two evils and quickly enlisted – at least they would get a £5 or £10 bounty for their troubles.

In a rare voice-from-the-ranks memoir, Private Robert Kirkwood of the 77th claims that he was one of the very first to enlist in Montgomery's Highlanders. A young cooper by trade living in the coastal town of Ayr, close by the Earl of Eglinton's estates, he "enlisted in his Majesty's 77th Regt. Of Foot commanded by Colonel Archibald Montgomery, in the latter end of the Year 1756 ... which was mostly composed of impress'd men from the Highlands." With no political axe to grind, Private Kirkwood simply states that the 77th Foot was not the voluntary and willing clan levy that Stewart and subsequent historians would have us believe.

An engraving of John Campbell, Earl of Loudoun and commander-in-chief in North America (1756–58), who felt that the 42nd's training on arrival in North America was not good enough. This portrait provides a very good example of Highland officer's dress, c.1756–60. (Library of Congress)

Kirkwood's compelling story also handily dispels another myth of the new Highland battalions being solely composed of Gaelic-speaking Highlanders, for the literate young man had no qualms in describing himself as a Lowlander and native of "North Britain." While the majority of Highland soldiers in all three regiments spoke Gaelic, a return of Kirkwood's regiment taken on its arrival in the New World shows that of the 1,060 rank and file listed, no less than 59 were annotated as "Lowland Scotch" to differentiate them from the true Highlanders. Even Stewart of Garth, though it probably pained him, admitted that in the raising of the 2nd Battalion of the 42nd Foot the following year, "eighteen Irishmen were enlisted at Glasgow by two officers anxious to obtain commissions."

Another common fallacy associated with the Highland regiments was that they were all brawny, giant warriors. In fact, recorded physical statistics of Jacobite prisoners compiled after the 1745 Uprising show the average height of the Highlanders to have been 5ft 4in., the "minimum" height requirement for the British Army. A quick look at the average height of Highlanders in the size roll of Major Clephane's 1757 recruits reveals that 44 out 130 men were actually less than 5ft 4in. tall, the shortest Highlander being 5ft 1in. and the tallest recruit measuring in at a towering 5ft 10in.

In essence, the Highlanders were raw, untrained recruits, no different from the laborers and weavers that flocked to the southern English regiments, with a few important exceptions. Rather than any special "warrior" gene or natural inclination for war, it was the Highlanders' language, dress, their level of physical fitness and endurance (demanded by their climate and environment), and their strong sense of ancestral honor, duty, and obligation that set them apart.

TRAINING

By no means fit for immediate Service
– LtCol Simon Fraser

The best-trained of the three Highland regiments was, without question, the 42nd Foot, a well-established unit and the most senior Highland regiment of the Georgian army, with its full slate of experienced officers and NCOs who were veterans and had campaigned in Flanders. However, the 2nd Division of 600 recruits, which would join them in the fall of 1756 at Fort Edward in upstate New York, would require extensive training, having had minimal time in Scotland to learn their arms drill or battalion drill before embarkation.

Lord Loudoun would report to the Duke of Cumberland after their arrival that his decision not to place them into any of the major forts for the winter of 1756–57 was predicated on this fact. Knowing the duke had last seen the regiment when it had soldiered gallantly with him in Flanders, Loudoun made special mention that the 42nd was no longer its former self. The old Highland regiment that had honorably acquitted itself at Fontenoy had "not near two hundred Men left of their old Ones." The duke predictably replied some months later that if the Highlanders had "but a Couple of Hundred of old Flanderkins in the Battalion" he would "look upon it as a pretty good one."

A

TRAINING: DRUMMERS OF THE ROYAL HIGHLAND REGIMENT, LAKE GEORGE CAMP, JULY 1759

A soft evening glow lights the southern end of Lake George, flanked by the Adirondack Mountains, as the drum major of the 1st Battalion, The Royal Highlanders, instructs three young drummers in the intricate beatings of the Georgian army. Long before the bugle was introduced during Napoleonic times, the entire 18th-century British Army was regulated by the beat of a drum. A 42nd orderly book entry gives us a basic idea of how the system worked in a brigade: "The drums of the regiment repeat the beats of the signal drum once, and the regiments make their movements from their own drums."

In this plate, a trio of drummers – a drummer of the grenadier company in his distinctive white bearskin flanked by two hat or "bonnet" company drummers – are wearing philabegs, the forerunner of the modern kilt. While drummers typically wore jackets of reversed-facing colors to distinguish them as musicians, these drummers' red jackets with blue collars and cuffs proudly proclaim the regiment's new "royal" status. The drums with red rims and blue backings are made from a wooden shell, their calf-skin drumheads held in place by the rims and tightened by ropes and leather lugs.

The drum major facing the three was the senior and most experienced drummer, who helped maintain the duty rosters for the regimental guard mountings. Lord John Murray took especial care to ensure his regimental drum majors and piper majors were dressed with sergeants' jackets trimmed with silver lace and silver shoulder knots. From his own personal correspondence in the Bagshawe Muniments, we also know that both senior regimental musicians would have worn grenadier caps with royal blue backings embroidered with silver lace. By contrast, the piper major wore a black bearskin cap with red feathers (see page 28) while the drum major and the grenadier company drummers of the two battalions wore white fur caps.

Regimental Orders from Fort Ontario in July 1760 give us an insight into some of the drum major's specific responsibilities: "The Drum Major to sett the drums of the regimt in repair immediately and he is to be out with them to practice till further orders from Trap beating to 10 o'clock and from 4 in the afternoon to 6 o'clock. He is to be answerable that the drums are properly dressed every morning before Trap beating." Aspiring drummers were also expected to pay the drum major for his patient tutelage: "The young drummers entertained since the regiment came to this country to pay the Drum-Major for teaching them…"

By contrast, the rank and file of the 77th and 78th Foot were completely raw, untrained levies when they were sent over, the only veterans in their ranks being some of their officers and NCOs. The ever-diplomatic Swiss professional, Col Henri Bouquet, reported to his superior that the newly arrived Montgomery Highlanders at Charles Town, while "on a very good Order, & will soon be formed under the Direction of such good Officers as the Colonel and Major Grant," were not properly trained. On top of this, its ability to receive training was hampered by the fact that they had "so great a Number of sick, and among them several Serjeants & Corporals." Bouquet assessed that "the Highlanders [were] quite raw men" and would not be employable as trained soldiers till at least the following year, 1758.

The commanding officer of the 78th Foot, Simon Fraser, was surprisingly frank in the assessment of his own regiment's standard of training upon arrival in North America in 1757. He admitted to Lord Loudoun that though his new regiment had all the outward appearances of his lordship's old regiment of the previous war, it would need much more time to train and to become accustomed to British Army ways. By the following spring he would report, after spending the winter months in Connecticut, that his troops were "in general healthy, young & well-built, but not tall. Highlanders seldom are."

Nonetheless, Fraser confessed that as trained British soldiers his young men were "not what I would have them" but they could "go through the platoon exercise pretty well … & they all march well & fire well at marks, which were the only things the cold would, for the greatest part of the winter, allow us to attempt." A 19th-century town historian in later years would attest to the Highlanders' prowess at shooting, claiming "Colonel Frasier's men amused themselves at times in shooting at the weathercock at the top of the Episcopal Church spire which they pierced several times."

When it came to describing his recently arrived recruits from Scotland, Col Fraser certainly didn't pull any punches:

In what I have said of the Regiment, I do not include the Additional Companies. They are not so good bodys of men, & till they came here most of their Arms never were taken out of the chests, so they know nothing. In their situation, I should be sorry to rest the Character of the regiment upon their behaviour, & should think it best for the Service to have them as they are at Halifax, or to exchange a few of their best men for a few of the worst of the Battalion, & taking all their Officers, carry 13 Companys of 70, and leave 300 bad men with a few Officers. As most of the Men of these 3 Companys are really by no means fit for immediate Service, I should be glad to receive your Orders about them…

An 18th-century view of Halifax with its harbor dominated by Citadel Hill as it would have appeared to all three Highland regiments who passed through at various times between 1757 and 1763. This contemporary view by J. F. W. Des Barres, a former officer of the 60th Foot (Royal Americans), is taken from the Dartmouth side of the harbor where the Fraser Highlanders encamped on their first arrival in North America, in the fall of 1757. (National Archives of Canada)

Even the 2nd Battalion of the Black Watch (2nd/42nd) sent to North America was so hastily assembled in Scotland that it had no training whatsoever before being sent over. Prior to departure the Highlanders learned they would not be joining their countrymen immediately, as British war strategy for the Americas had expanded to include an attempt to seize lucrative French possessions in the Caribbean. The 2nd/42nd Foot was assigned to Gen Hopson's 1759 expedition against the French islands of Martinique and Guadeloupe, and John Grant, an 18-year-old officer leading a platoon of 25 young Highlanders not much older than himself, confessed in his memoirs that his raw untrained recruits only had "their arms deliver'd to them the day" before they were asked to go into combat. He also admitted that, before that day, he had never "commanded men under arms."

Luckily for John Grant, during his recruiting days at Aberdeen he had made the effort of attending "the drills of the Regt. quartered there and had seen the manner of loading." The day before an assault landing was ordered against Fort St Louis on Guadeloupe, the young officer, assisted by his sergeant, showed his men "the way to load, describing the ramming down the cartridge. When I came to examine [their weapons] I found that 15 out of 25 in my platoon had chosen to put the ball in foremost."

Typically, the firing and loading drills as well as platoon, company, and battalion training were the purview of the battalion commander. In order to be able to function at a much higher tactical level in the British army, or in tandem with the Royal Navy on combined operations such as the assault landings at Louisburg (1758), Québec (1759), and Martinique and Havana (1762), the Highlanders of all three regiments underwent collective training and rehearsals organized by their respective generals.

In sum, Highland recruits started to learn the rudiments of firearms drill on board their transport ships en route to North America, or during their first winter in garrison towns or cities. As the regiments collected together for major operations, they would undergo further training together as brigades as well as any specialized training required for the mission they were assigned.

DRESS, APPEARANCE, AND EQUIPMENT

That the battalion may appear to the best advantage
– *42nd Regimental Orderly Book*

Although James Thompson neglected to tell us much about his Highland dress, one of his company commander's orderly books, as well as several of the 42nd Foot, have survived and give us excellent detail on how Highlanders' dress and equipment evolved during the course of the war in North America.

The dress and weapons of a Highland regiment were, without a doubt, the most distinguishing features that set them apart from a standard Georgian line regiment of the day. The promise of going to war in the garb of their forefathers and wielding Highland weapons cannot be understated, for even the bards mention this great honor being accorded to the young soldiers going off to fight in the Seven Years' War. Owing to the soldiers acquitting themselves honorably overseas, one poet went so far as to predict that the much-loved native dress would be restored to all Highlanders on their triumphant return. On the other hand, if the ten Highland regiments that were eventually raised for service during the Seven Years' War had been initially told they could not wear the belted plaid or broadswords on their hips, John Prebble argues that "clansmen would have turned their backs upon William Pitt's patriotic appeal."

Ironically, the Proscription Act, outwardly designed to break the obstinately aggressive spirit of the clans, astutely included a pertinent clause stating that the

coveted kilt could still be worn, but only by men "as shall be employed as officers and soldiers in the King's Forces." The lost prestige and coveted dress and weapons of the Highlander were thus transferred to a very select few – those willing to don the redcoat.

From head to toe, with the exception of the king's redcoat, the Highland soldier sported traditional clothing, and this privilege was a key part in fostering and maintaining his sense of identity and belonging. On his head was the "tam" or blue bonnet, the Highlander's distinctive headdress worn by soldiers and civilians of the Highlands alike. Similar to the universal beret of today, it varied slightly in form and size from district to district, but in the Highland regiments finally found a form that was standardized by sharp-eyed adjutants. Above the left ear, the Highlanders wore a black ribbon cockade on the bonnet headband that served as an anchor for their black bearskin tufts, "not to be more than 5 inches in length" and termed "the Hair cockade."

Hose (caddis in Gaelic, meaning "striped") were the woolen stockings worn by the Highlander and usually woven with a standardized pattern of diagonal stripes, the most common being red crossing and mingling with white. On occasion the 42nd, however, used the "Government Sett" tartan to make hose, and Fraser's troops at Québec in 1759–60 were forced to cut up captured French blankets to replace worn-out hose when their new clothing did not arrive before the onset of winter.

Highlanders wore standard regulation army shoes of black leather, made to a common pattern and fastened with a brass buckle. When issued, they were not form-fitted to either the right or left foot. Soldiers were commonly ordered to change their shoes around every other day in order to prevent them from "running crooked" and thus wearing out sooner.

Many Highland soldiers of all three regiments adopted the Indian moccasin for wear while in North America on campaign, especially the light infantry companies. The moccasin closely resembled their Highland pump or laced heel-less shoe known as a cuaran worn back in Scotland. The latter was made of untanned deerskin or cowhide worn with the hairy side out and fastened by criss-cross thongs over the instep and ankles. This lightweight shoe was ideal for moving swiftly and nimbly over the hills and countryside, but wore out quickly, as did its North American counterpart.

Jackets

Jackets or coats of Highland regiments resembled those of their countrymen and remained short throughout the Seven Years' War. They were initially single-breasted, with small cuffs and cropped skirts known as a "jacket" (later a "coatee"), a pattern common throughout Scotland and not confined to the Highlands. Those ranked major and above wore lapels on their jackets displaying the regimental facing as early as the 1740s. Company officers (captains, lieutenants, and ensigns), according to 42nd Foot orderly books, did not adopt lapels until February 1760.

While campaigning in the wilderness, experienced officers, ever-conscious of Indian and Canadian marksmen, took measures as early as 1758 to ensure they closely resembled their men by discarding their sashes and gorgets, carrying muskets known as "fuzees," and wearing their older unlaced regimental coats without lapels. Lieutenant John Grant remembered that the 42nd Foot were experienced veterans by the time they reached the siege of Havana in 1762, freely admitting "we were equipped in jackets without lace made to resemble soldiers."

Men's coats were issued on a scale of one new coat per year, the older, faded coat usually being converted into a red waistcoat, the newer coats being reserved for reviews or guard mountings. Many orderly book entries directed that only old coats were to be worn on fatigue parties out of camp or on campaign. Every spring, each Highland regiment went through the necessary process of rotating worn-out coats and plaids and replacing them with the new, a process that demanded trained tailors assigned to every company.

One could tell the difference between a Highland officer and an enlisted man at a distance merely by the color of his coat. The former, plus sergeants, wore scarlet coats of finer cloth while lower ranks wore a brick-red jacket. In addition, other badges of rank were added to the coat or worn over it to distinguish officers and sergeants from the men. These included a crimson sash worn over the left shoulder by officers (netted silk) and sergeants (red worsted wool), quantities of gold and silver lace around buttonholes (sergeants wore a narrower silver lace, almost piping), cuffs, collars, lapels and waistcoats, as well as gold and silver shoulder knots or aiguillettes that hung off the right shoulder.

Corporals were only distinguished by a right shoulder-knot of white or regimental facing color. In addition, officers wore a silver or brass gorget about their necks – the last vestige of medieval armor now reduced to small engraved crescent bearing the king's royal cipher and the regimental number. The gorget was suspended below the throat with a ribbon of the regimental color.

Belted plaid

All Highland regiments that served in North America wore the belted plaid or the *feileadh mór* that consisted of 12 yards of double-width woolen tartan or cloth. The plaid was always worn over other clothes. A long shirt at the very least would be worn under the plaid, the former being tied between the legs and serving as underwear. Other items of clothing would then be added, such as

Opposite page A private soldier of the 78th Foot wears (from the top down) a blue bonnet with black bearskin cockade; a white shirt under a short Highland pattern coat with off-white facings; full plaids; waist belt with cartridge bellybox, a dirk, a sporran and bayonet; an issue backsword with shoulder belt; an issue Highland pistol; red-and-white diced hose held up with red garters; and black shoes with brass buckles. A modern reconstruction by Douglas Anderson. (David M. Stewart Museum Library, Montréal)

© G.A. EMBLETON

All Highland regiments that served in North America wore the belted plaid or the *feileadh mór* (literally "big wrap"). In order for a soldier to put on his plaid, he would lie down on the "kelted" plaid, the top edge just above his head with the other end level with a point just above his knee. He would then wrap the plaid about his lower half and fasten with a black belt. Standing up, the lower belted half formed the kilt proper; the extra material hanging out the back of his belt was then gathered and fastened at the left shoulder by a shoulder button in order to leave the right sword arm free. (Illustration by Gerry Embleton from Osprey's Men-at-Arms 118: *The Jacobite Rebellions 1689–1745* by Michael Barthorp)

hose, shoes, and jacket or, in the case of North America, leggings. The plaid was usually discarded before any physical exertion as it was bulky, especially when wet, and could be inconvenient for movement in the wilderness, commonly becoming entangled with the undergrowth.

The plaid quickly became a multi-purpose piece of kit for Highland soldiers in North America: a blanket at night, a cloak for inclement weather to protect the soldier and his weapon, a stretcher for carrying the wounded, and a knapsack or blanket roll for carrying provisions on long wilderness marches. In 1759, on Gen Amherst's expedition against Fort Ticonderoga and Crown Point, both battalions of the 42nd Foot were ordered "to embark in their leggings" with their "plaids well packed except such as are intended for sails." In November 1759, John Grant recounts in his journal that they were using a plaid for a sail to cross Lake Oneida from west to east, when a sudden squall threatened to capsize the boat and he was forced to slash the plaid with his dirk to save the boat and crew.

The usual rule of thumb in the Highland regiments was to convert plaids into kilts or philabegs (or, in Gaelic, *feileadh beag* meaning "little wrap") after one year of wear, the wearing of the bulkier belted plaid usually reserved for dress parades and reviews only. On ceremonial occasions, such as when the 42nd Foot was drawn up in three ranks in Montréal in 1761, we find the older faded plaids and waistcoats of the soldiers given to the center rank men to wear, while the newer and brighter plaids were worn by the front and rear ranks so "that the battalion may appear to the best advantage." After two years, the plaid became the soldier's personal property, but the commanding officer still exercised some control over its disposal. The price, if retained for regimental use, was settled on by the soldiers themselves taking a vote supervised by the sergeants.

The gradual adoption of the philabeg or kilt as everyday work dress and an alternative to the belted plaid in North America by the Highland regiments is recorded as early as 1758 in letters and orderly books of the day. At first, the little kilt was made from worn-out plaids, 3–3½ yards usually sufficient for that purpose. The following year saw little kilts as the accepted basic dress for camp duty, fatigues, and bateaux work, but most had acquired breeches over the winter in upstate New York.

The sporran or *sporran molash* (Gaelic for "hairy purse") was a personal item of kit for both officers and men. It was a field item only and not worn on guard or parades, and it was not standard issue and therefore not uniform in appearance. Essentially it was a hanging frontal pouch for storing money, pipes, tobacco, or other small personal items. According to Thompson, in Scotland badger skin or otter skin was used to make the purses initially; later in Canada, some soldiers acquired beaver purses.

Dirk and pommel

The standard weaponry for the Highlander, with the exception of his musket, set him apart from his English counterpart. One of the deadliest weapons in a Highlander's arsenal was his dirk, a dagger that had evolved purely and simply for fighting and killing with deadly efficiency. It was a personal and thus non-issue weapon and hence reflected the owner's tastes as well as means. Worn on the right hip to counterbalance the broadsword on the left, a Highlander would draw it with his left hand after he had drawn his backsword with the right.

Dirk blades on average were from 10–18in. long – the upper length was usually a good indication that the weapon had been made from a cut-down sword. Grenadier Thompson of the 78th Foot, while in winter quarters at Stratford, CT, in 1757, confessed that he:

> …was sadly off for want of a Dirk, and coaxed our regimental armourer to make a blade of one out of a sword blade I had got… He said he would try his hand at it, and accordingly set to work – he found great difficulty in shaping it on account of the hardness of the steel, but at length he continued to finish it tolerably well. I myself carved the handle and got a silversmith to mount it from a pattern which I got for him.

All officers and sergeants, at least in the 78th Foot, were required to wear dirks on duty, as Thompson tells us: "Sergeant Fraser of our Regiment, having lent his dirk to one of the Officers of his Company and having occasion to go somewhere or other, on duty, he borrowed mine…"

Backswords

One of the most highly prized weapons worn by a Highland soldier was his backsword. There were basically two types of Highland sword found in the Highland regiments. The first and most common was the enlisted man's

Made from a cut-down backsword blade marked Andreia Ferara, this dirk has a handle fully carved with intertwined Celtic designs and an engraved brass plate pommel cap. A dirk of this quality would have been carried either by an officer or a private soldier of personal means. (Private collection)

sword, which was a patterned-sword design used as early as 1745. Supplied by the colonels of the regiment for their soldiers, and deducted in off-reckonings from their pay, these poor-quality weapons cost about eight shillings and sixpence each.

The second type of sword was personal property, not issued by the regiment, and typically carried by officers, NCOs, and privates from good families. These were traditional and ornate Scottish backswords, masterpieces of the swordmaker's art, with two-sided blades usually imported from the steelmakers of Solingen in Germany, though some came from French forges. Lengths varied from about 28 to 38in. The basket hilts, however, were crafted in Glasgow and Stirling by the Hammerman Guilds, each with their own distinctive marks, patterns, and decorative flourishes.

Two fine examples of backswords, the more ornate and highly finished sword on the left a personally owned weapon (probably a family heirloom) typically carried by an officer or NCO, while the plain but sturdy Drury sword on the right was the standard army issue made for the private soldier. (Private collection)

Highland pistols and carbines

All three Highland regiments that served in North America were issued with all-metal Highland-pattern pistols, but many officers and NCOs brought their own personal weapons with them. Private soldiers were issued regulation pistols that were all-steel or iron, barrels unblued, with ram's horn or scroll butts and steel ramrods. Most were engraved with the regimental and battalion numbers on top of the barrels.

B **TICONDEROGA ASSAULT, 1758**

At the desperate Battle of Ticonderoga, fought on July 8, 1758, only one regiment – the Black Watch – penetrated the earthen log defenses of the French lines built across the heights of Carillon. The 42nd Foot's desire to close with and destroy its French enemy at Ticonderoga was so focused and so complete, that the men were only persuaded to withdraw after they had run out of ammunition. The Black Watch at Ticonderoga suffered 65 percent casualties in a single day's action, 647 men out of a total strength of 1,000 all ranks, a loss unsurpassed by any other regiment in 18th-century North American history.

"The Highlanders attacked with the greatest fury," recalled a French officer, "and this attack threatened real danger." Général Montcalm, sword in hand, marched quickly at the head of the reserve grenadiers just in time to see screaming Highlanders jumping over the parapet led by a large 6ft-tall Scot wielding his broadsword with deadly effect.

In this plate, we see the CaptLt John Campbell from Duneaves, leading his men against the French grenadiers. Given a battlefield promotion for gallantry at Fontenoy, Campbell and a handful of Highlanders at Ticonderoga forced their way over the entrenchment walls in the Bearn regiment's sector, but were quickly bowled over and bayoneted in the counterattack led by Montcalm. Campbell and a dozen of his men were killed, while the remaining seven Highlanders were given quarter and allowed to surrender.

We can also see the back of the French defenses at Ticonderoga in this plate, hurriedly constructed in just three days by Montcalm's entire army. It consisted of a log wall stretching and zig-zagging the width of the heights, 7–8ft high, constructed from very large logs (trimmed flat on the top and bottom) lying lengthwise atop an earthen bank thrown up from a ditch in front facing the enemy. To the front of the wooden ramparts, green trees and branches camouflaged and masked the actual size and strength of the French defenses from the British until it was too late.

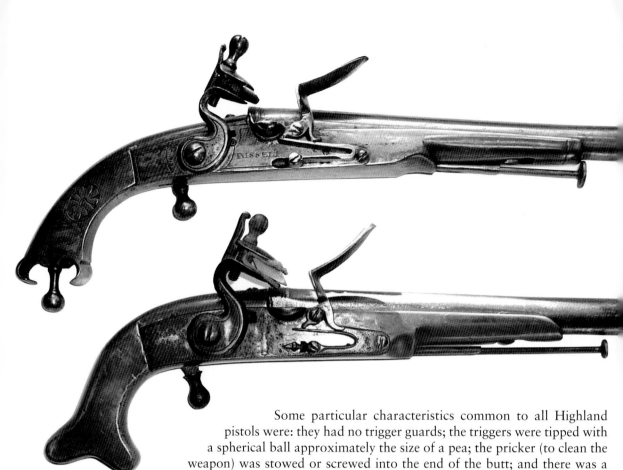

Two Highland pistols, both issued to the Royal Highland Regiment, the Black Watch. The top pistol is all-steel with a ram's horn pattern butt, made by Bissell, and marked on the barrel "R.H.R." The second pistol with its bronze stock and scroll pattern butt was made by John Waters of Birmingham (worked 1766–88). His initials "I.W." are on the steel barrel, with the government proofmarks including the crown over "GR" (King George III). (Private Collection)

Some particular characteristics common to all Highland pistols were: they had no trigger guards; the triggers were tipped with a spherical ball approximately the size of a pea; the pricker (to clean the weapon) was stowed or screwed into the end of the butt; and there was a belt-hook or slide affixed to the reverse side of the pistol. Only one pistol, usually 12in. in length, was issued to each man, and it was carried on a narrow strap slung from the right shoulder so that the weapon hung under the left armpit.

The 42nd Foot, first to arrive in North America, came equipped with regulation King's Pattern 1742 Long Land muskets characterized by a double-bridle lock, walnut stock, a 46-in. long, .75-cal. round barrel and a wooden rammer. By contrast, the 77th and 78th Foot arrived in North America in 1757 equipped with 37-in. carbines with iron ramrods. Fraser informed Lord Loudoun in April 1758 that his regimental arms were "the Carabines the horse had before they were reduced to Dragoons, and are excellent Arms in every respect, but that they are rather slight for hard use…"

The Highlander carbines were similar to those issued to the artillery, and we find in various orders of the day those same carbines being reissued to the various regimental light infantry companies. For example, before the 1758 Louisburg campaign, the Highlanders of the three untrained 78th Additional companies of the 78th left behind in Halifax were ordered to exchange their carbines for Brown Bess muskets, one-for-one, with the light infantry of Major George Scott's Provisional Battalion. Rifles were a limited-issue firearm. The 42nd received ten rifles for its best marksmen, as did seven other regiments, just prior to the Battle of Ticonderoga (July 8, 1758). These 80 rifles came from a batch of 300 rifled carbines, each fitted with bayonets and steel rammers. They were brought to North America by Col James Prevost of the Royal Americans.

BELIEF AND BELONGING

Strangers to their own army

The strong *esprit de corps* shown by the Highland regiments and their soldiery in the French-Indian War stemmed directly from key elements of their Highland culture. The traditional dress and Highland weapons were merely physical manifestations of a fierce pride shaped by a highly developed sense of honor and kinship. Coming from a strong oral tradition that placed heavy importance on the clan bard and clan piper, this sense of *Còir* ("what is proper") and *Ceart* ("what is right and just") underscored most of the Highland soldier's actions in everyday military service, and is only captured in their songs, poetry, and storytelling. Common to all of this, of course, was the rich, resonant Gaelic language of their ancestors.

A painting Robert Griffing shows a Highland soldier performing a sword dance on the drill square of the captured Fort Carillon, renamed Ticonderoga on its capture by MajGen Jeffery Amherst in 1759. It was a matter of personal pride and honor for the Highland dancer not to touch the blades of the swords while performing the intricate footwork of the dance. A seated Iroquois warrior accompanies the piper with a native drum similar to the Celtic *bodhran* or hand drum. (Robert Griffing & Paramount Press)

SPECIALIST HIGHLAND SOLDIERS

(1) Grenadier Corporal, 78th Foot

A grenadier corporal of Fraser's Highlanders (78th Foot) disembarks from a boat at Louisburg, June 8, 1758. Typically, the grenadiers were the tallest and strongest men of the regiment, the elite shock troops that led the charge, hence their special headdress to differentiate them from the regular "bonnet" companies – the high grenadier bearskin cap with an off-white front plate and red embroidery made them look taller and more imposing. His hair is clubbed with a black ribbon and he wears full plaids. A white worsted knot hangs from his right shoulder to denote his rank.

The grenadier name derived from the function they had performed in the 17th century – lobbing hand grenades over enemy walls and entrenchments prior to the final assault. Army commanders would customarily organize the regimental grenadier companies into a special assault battalion which they could then use to spearhead attacks on critical vital points. While this practice deprived the regiments of their best and biggest soldiers, commanding officers recognized that it was for the common good of the army.

At Louisburg, Wolfe specially requested that the Highland grenadiers be added to the "Four eldest companies" leading the first wave of the assault. Accordingly, Sgt James Thompson's company suffered the heaviest casualties, a single cannonball killing Thompson's best friend and company commander, Charles Baillie, as well as the company's senior lieutenant and sergeant.

(2) Pioneer, 77th Foot

The Pioneers (or "Hatchet Men" as they were commonly known) were the artificers of the regiment, men adept with axes, saws and hammers. Rather than unskilled navvies, they represented the skilled artisans of the regiment (carpenters, wheelwrights, coopers) who received extra pay for their work and were usually found taking a leading role in erecting field defenses, siege works, and supervising the construction of fortifications such as Fort Ontario at Oswego or Crown Point on Lake Champlain.

They were also the first infantry soldiers that Royal Engineers employed as overseers, and, because of their elite status and special duties, they were also allowed to wear the same bearskin caps as the grenadiers and the grenadier company drummers. Here, a pioneer of the 77th (Montgomery's) wearing a bearskin with green backing and white embroidery takes time out from a march, resting on his 7-in. "eared" camp axe. He wears work gauntlets, a russet leather apron over his kilt, and protective leather gaiters over his hose and shoes. Pioneers were, in effect, the regiment's own personal corps of engineers and the daily beating for work parties to assemble was known as "The Pioneer's March."

(3) Piper Major, 2nd/42nd Foot

For many years there has been much discussion on whether pipers wore uniforms or not during the French-Indian War. Most accounts speculate that pipers were non-combatants retained on the personal payroll of their respective company commanders. But recent research has revealed that on its raising, the 77th ordered uniform coats comparable to those issued to sergeants especially for their company pipers, and Lord John Murray's correspondence to LtCol Grant in the Bagshawe Muniments clearly shows that he dressed his pipers (four per battalion) not only in the best silver-laced scarlet jackets, but outfitted each with black bearskin caps with silver embroidery and red feathers.

Here Owen McIntyre, the piper major of the 2nd Battalion, The Royal Highlanders, plays his Great Highland bagpipes. A royal blue pipe banner flies from one of his old fashioned bell-shaped drones, the banner a special present sent by a proud Lord John to each of his battalions to mark their new "royal" status granted in 1758. The battalion number appears in the top right quarter, while in the center the regimental number in Roman numerals is surmounted by the same royal cipher authorized for use on the regiment's colors. Colonels of regiments were forbidden to put their own coats-of-arms or devices on flags or banners.

All pipers were gifted musicians, many from traditional piping families such as the MacCrimmons, MacArthurs, or MacIntyres, where composition and playing techniques were passed down from generation to generation. In olden times, clan pipers were men of high musical attainments and were accorded near deity status. The courses of training they underwent, lasting in most cases over several years at piping schools, turned out finished performers. A good piper was not easily made and as the old Gaelic phrase put it – "Into the making of a piper go seven years of his own learning and seven generations before."

Bards

Grenadier Sgt James Thompson, the storyteller, was more than just an NCO of the regiment. Though not officially on the establishment as such, he was a throwback to the age of true clan regiments, a vestige of the ancient Celtic bards, who during battles acted as heralds and walked with complete immunity between the warring septs. Their sacred role – to guard the clan's honor during negotiations – had given them nearly the same "pit & gallows" power the chiefs possessed.

There were many noted poets and composers of song within the ranks of the 42nd, 77th, and Thompson's regiment, the best known in the latter being one Corporal Iain Campbell whose song "At the Siege of Quebec, 1759" remains the most stirring, graphic, and emotional record of the 78th's deeds during that eventful campaign. In the Erse oral culture, bards were the "collective memory" of the clan, the principal repository for the clan's history and genealogy. More than herald, historian, lawyer, and storyteller, the bard was the composer of new songs, weaving the living clansfolk into their clan's past legacy and future fortunes. A bard's inclusion of a clansman's name in a song was a life-changing experience. Not only did it place him into the oral history of his kinsmen forever, but clothed a man with honor for the rest of his waking life – no small matter in the Highlands, where the worst Gaelic curse one could bestow upon another person was: "May your name be forgotten forever."

Pipers

Perhaps some of the most iconic and inspiring figures of the Highland regiments that served in North America were their pipers, playing the "outlawed" pipes and the traditional music of the clans. From the outset of the 1745 Uprising, it was well known that the piper's role was essentially a martial one, marching into battle alongside his comrades and encouraging them to deeds of valor with the rant of his pipes. Indeed, court trials after the rebellion noted that a Highland unit "never marched without its piper" and therefore the player and his pipes were considered "Instruments of War" in the eyes of the British authorities. Many pipers were thus found guilty of being rebels and executed or deported for taking up arms against their king.

Pipers were not initially on the regimental establishments, though the 1758 Royal Warrant authorizing the creation of a second battalion for the 42nd Foot specifically authorized one piper instead of a fifer to each of the battalions' grenadier companies. Bagpipes were the personal property of the pipers that came to North America with their regiments. Additional pipers were most certainly taken on as drummers, who were paid more than a private and considered as junior NCOs. A 42nd orderly book reveals that on April 10, 1759, "Peter McIntyre pipper in Capt. MacNeill's company is for the future to be on the footing of a Drum and to be subsisted accordingly." The same entry also announced that "Owen McIntyre pipper in the Grenadier Company is appointed pipper-major and is this day to receive the clothing accordingly."

Pipers were responsible for playing tunes before and during the battle to inspire the men to greater deeds. After the battle they were also expected to compose laments to honor the fallen, or in happier circumstances, to commemorate the brave exploits of the clan or a particular warrior much along the same lines as a clan bard would do verbally. As the piper had been an integral part of the martial culture of the Highlands, embodied in the earlier clan regiments, so he became an important beacon of cultural identity and traditional belonging for the Highland soldiers serving in North America.

Language

From the outset of the French-Indian War, British authorities were aware that one of the biggest cultural hurdles for the Highlanders in the British Army would be operating in the English language on a daily basis. Thus it was preferable, though not mandatory, that all Highland officers and NCOs be fluent in both languages as well as able to read and write in English. Lord Barrington had certainly recognized this requirement in the raising of the two new Highland battalions.

While language certainly was not a large problem in the 42nd and 77th Foot, which were commanded by well-educated officers and NCOs from the loyal clans, James Thompson's regiment was a different story. The 78th comprised a large number of former Jacobites, and thus some NCOs were only able to converse in the Gaelic, while all of the private soldiers were unilingual.

For example, one of the first casualties of the 78th to occur in North America was a private soldier killed at Halifax, Nova Scotia. While returning to the tent lines, he was challenged in English by a sentry. "With his hair hanging loose and wrapped up in a dark-coloured plaid ... he looked like an Indian," concluded a Scottish officer, and was shot down after not responding to several challenges to stop. The officer attributed the unfortunate incident to the newly arrived Highlander's being "raw and unexperienced" with "very few conversant in, or able to talk English." It could be said that not only were the Highlanders strangers in a strange land, but strangers to their own army.

For bilingual sergeants like Thompson in the 78th Foot, communication meant extra effort. "I spoke English and could write in a tolerably fair hand," but "there was a difficulty among the Sergeants of our Company in getting

Here in Robert Griffing's painting *The Intimidators*, three British-allied Delaware warriors eye a young Highland sentry at Fort Ligonier in the Laurel Highlands, about 50 miles east of Fort Duquesne. The 77th Foot helped build Ligonier in 1758–59 and the crucial Forbes Road connecting it to several other forts guarding the line of communications to Fort Pitt and back to Carlisle and Philadelphia. (Robert Griffing & Paramount Press).

Above Many songs and tunes of the Highlanders, composed while soldiering in North America, have survived and reveal a keen pride in their accomplishments, but, at the same time, a deep longing for "hame". This painting entitled *Long Way from Home* by Robert Griffing evokes that rich oral tradition of music and songs used by the Highlanders to help pass away the loneliness of garrison duty on the frontier. (Robert Griffing and Paramount Press)

Above right With Fort Duquesne just visible in the distance, a piper of the Montgomery Highlanders plays in an attempt to rally Major James Grant's disorganized raiding force on September 13, 1758. Bagpipes were of two kinds: the two-droned bagpipe (seen here) and the three-droned Great Highland bagpipes, which saw the addition of a third bass drone. (Robert Griffing & Paramount Press)

them to take orders, for they could hardly write." Thompson's biggest chore was Duncan McPhee, a large man who had been a notorious outlaw back in the Highlands and had caught the eye of Gen Wolfe several times for gallant deeds. Promoted to sergeant at Louisburg, McPhee could hardly speak a word of English and "gave me a great deal of trouble from his not knowing a single letter in the Alphabet!"

Racism

The comparison of the Highlander to natives of North America during the French-Indian War was quite commonplace. One of the earliest recorded impressions of the Highlanders in North America likening them (because of their different dress and language) to the "savages" of North America appeared in the Scot's Magazine back home. It reported that upon the 42nd Foot's arrival at Albany "an incredible number of Indians flocked to them from all quarters," and interpreters were subsequently "chosen on either side" so they could effectively communicate. "From the surprising resemblance in the manner of their dress and the great similitude of their language," a somewhat tongue-in-cheek Edinburgh editor wrote, "the Indians concluded they were anciently one and the same people, and most cordially received them as brethren, which may be productive of effects beneficial to the British interest."

Stewart of Garth would give the same, but heavily edited, version of the letter in his book *Sketches of the Highlanders*, but paraphrased it to distort its original sense. His version reads: "When the Highlanders landed they were caressed by all ranks and order of men, but more particularly by the Indians. On the march to Albany, the Indians flocked from all quarters to see the strangers, who, they believed, were of the same extraction as themselves and therefore received them as brothers."

Garth obviously didn't like the second part of the original letter, with its Lowlander "wink-wink" racist overtones that portrayed the Highlanders as the British equivalent of a savage. William Amherst, the brother of MajGen Jeffery Amherst commanding at Louisburg, reported in his journal that the enemy certainly regarded them as "savages" and had been terrified by the Highlanders' sudden appearance and aggressiveness at the landings. Four or five days after the assault, groups of French regulars who had hidden from the Highlanders in the woods were still trickling in to give themselves up.

"They told us they stood in the utmost awe of Our Savages, & did not dare show themselves for fear of them," he proudly wrote a week after the landings. Mindful of the French slur, Amherst hastened to add that the Highlanders, in his opinion, were actually "most excellent troops" as well as "intrepid, subordinate, sober & indefatigable."

Above Some aspects of the Woodland Indian culture encountered by Highlanders were viewed as primitive and even barbaric. For some of the soldiers, such as Robert Kirkwood of the 77th Foot who was captured by Shawnee in 1758, and thus experienced it first-hand, it was a different story. This painting called *Life and Death* brings out the sense of independence and fortitude Kirkwood found among his captors as two warriors traverse the Adirondack "Highlands" above Lake George. (Robert Griffing & Paramount Press)

CONDITIONS OF SERVICE

This is very severe duty.
– Lieutenant Malcolm Fraser, 78th Foot

Accommodations

Accommodations for the Highland soldier were as varied as the many different theaters of war. They were billeted in forts, taverns, townhouses and grand estates while being recruited in Scotland or while in transit through Ireland on their way to Cork, the ultimate collection and embarkation point for all army transatlantic convoys bound for North America.

Left This 18th-century painting by Lieutenant Thomas Davies of the Royal Artillery depicts MajGen Jeffery Amherst's army encamped at the southern edge of Lake George in June 1759, poised to move against the French forts of Carillon (Ticonderoga) and St Frédéric (Crown Point) to the north. With over 10,000 men in camp, the population of this small canvas city was only surpassed by that of Philadelphia (23,800), New York (18,000), and Boston (15,600). (Fort Ticonderoga Museum)

Above The British built large Vauban-style forts, complete with barrack accommodations for their soldiers, at strategic locations throughout North America, usually at the confluence of important and well-traveled waterways. In a painting entitled *Fort Pitt under Siege, 1763* by Robert Griffing, we see the scope and size of the fortifications at the Ohio Forks, which the Black Watch would garrison from 1763 to 1767. (Robert Griffing & Paramount Press)

Below Built by carpenters and masons of the 42nd Foot and the Royal Americans in 1764, the Bouquet Redoubt at Fort Pitt is now the oldest-standing roofed structure in western Pennsylvania. Artisans installed a small sundial on one of the walls, its plate engraved with the regimental symbols of the soldiers: a thistle for the Highlanders and a rattlesnake for the Royal Americans. (Library of Congress)

On arrival in North America, the Highlanders were usually assigned to quarters provided by various colonial governments or expected to use their tents if the weather was amenable. For example, in June 1756 the 42nd Foot arriving at Albany in upstate New York colony was kept on board its transports on the Hudson River for two days until billets could be found for its Highlanders in the town. The *Pennsylvania Gazette* reported that they were housed with the residents "in twos, threes and fours," as they had brought no tents with them, the majority of their regimental baggage due to come over with the 2nd Division being recruited in Scotland. When the regiment was up to full strength and all the tentage had arrived, the Black Watch were sent to Fort Edward in September 1756. As winter closed in, they returned to the Mohawk River Valley and were billeted in the town of Schenectady and outlying farms.

By contrast, the arrival of the 77th Foot in Charles Town in September 1759 was not attended with any concerted effort to make the Scots welcome, and the 1,100 Highland soldiers were initially "Quarter'd in a finished Church without Windows, in Damp Store-houses upon the Quay, and in empty Houses where most of the Men were obliged to ly upon the Ground without Straw or any sort of Covering." Not surprisingly, within days "immediate Sickness was the consequence of such a reception after so long a Voyage," reported Montgomery and other field officers in a report to Lord Loudoun after some months in garrison. The 77th had disembarked at the beginning of September, a healthy battalion with only 16 men sick, but by the end of the month "there were above 500 sick." Of this number 60 men died over the next three months, and "still greater Numbers must have perish'd if some of the Inhabitants of this Town had not out of Compassion received near 200 of them into their Houses."

While the Highlanders mounted guards or helped build batteries around the harbor in the cooler air of October, the parsimonious South Carolinian Assembly deliberated whether or not they should build the British regulars a 1,000-man barracks. By the end of October they had voted monies for that purpose, but then promptly adjourned for a month "without giving any Directions about providing the Troops with Beding [sic] and other Barrack Necessities." The Highlanders were outraged in November when "The Gentlemen of the Assembly who were well-acquainted with the Severity of the weather during the Winter season" returned and were "pleased to order a Blanket for two Men in a Country where the most covetous Planter finds it in his Interest to allow One to the most despicable slave."

The wrangling over blankets, firewood and candle allocations, separate quarters, and allowances for officers and the building of a hospital for the garrison sick

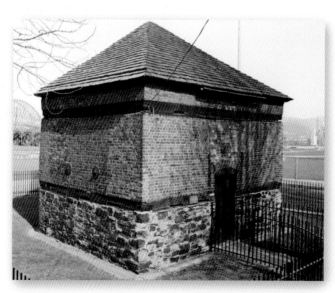

Dutch-style houses lining the main street of Albany (formerly Fort Orange of the colony of New Netherlands) in which the Highlanders of the 42nd Foot were first billeted on their arrival in the summer of 1756. (Library of Congress)

continued unabated into the next year and, remarkably, right up until the day of the 77th's departure for Pennsylvania the following spring.

When away from established towns and cities, the Highlanders and other regiments would erect their own canvas cities. These could be extremely large. The tented camp in which the two battalions of the 42nd and 77th Foot found themselves at Lake George, NY, in the summer of 1759 prior to Amherst's advance against Fort Ticonderoga and Crown Point in 1759, was the fourth largest "city" in the Thirteen Colonies.

In more established semi-permanent camps, rude huts would be constructed, while in captured cities such as Québec, the 78th Highlanders billeted in the ruined houses and buildings were forced to repair their winter accommodations before they were habitable. The practical grenadier sergeant, James Thompson of Fraser's Highlanders, had an eye for construction and "made choice of a little house in the Esplanade although it was scarcely inhabitable from the number of our shells that had fallen through it." Thompson put his Highlanders to work and "contriv'd to get a number of little jobs done towards making it passibly comfortable for the men, and for my own part I got Hector Munro, who was a joiner by trade to knock up a kind of Cabinet (as the Canadians call it) in one corner of the house for myself."

Everyday tasks

Thompson gives us a good idea of the more routine tasks and outpost duties he and his fellow Highlanders were called upon to perform while in garrison or on campaign. Of these tasks, mounting guard was perhaps the most common but essential duty, but regiments were also typically called upon to assist in road-building through the North American wilderness, construct new forts to guard strategic waterways or portages, or work as common laborers in the siege lines. The 77th Foot assigned to Gen John Forbes' 1758 expedition to capture Fort Duquesne on the Forks of the Ohio found themselves working alongside their American counterparts in the provincial forces, learning to swing an axe and construct corduroy roads.

In the vast and often uncharted forests of North America, just getting an army in a position to fight was a major achievement. In his 1758 expedition against Fort Duquesne on the Forks of the Ohio, Gen John Forbes had to blaze a road for his army through the extremely rugged terrain of western Pennsylvania. Providing the raw labor were the Highlanders of the 77th Foot, the Royal Americans, and provincial soldiers. (Dover Pictorial Archives.)

In order to keep track of weaponry in the various Highland regiments, the barrels or hilts of pistols and swords were engraved by the regimental armorers with the company number or letter, followed by the company number assigned to a soldier. Thus the pistol shown here belonged to soldier number 47 of the 10th Company of the 2nd Battalion, 42nd Foot. The Drury sword belonged to soldier 41 of A Company (the colonel's company) of the 42nd Foot. (Private collection)

Thompson's regiment found itself assigned to garrison duty in the Mohawk River Valley the winter of 1758/59, and the four Highlander companies assigned to the new and incomplete Fort Stanwix encamped outside until they finished building the barracks that would house them for the winter. Over the course of the winter, their commanding officer, James Clephane, an old Flanders veteran who had served with the Dutch Scots Brigade, would keep his young Highlanders busy digging the dry ditch encompassing the walls and bastions. When the ground was too frozen to dig further, they constructed a palisade running through it at its lowest point to impede would-be attackers, and then built a ravelin in front of the main gate to protect it from a surprise rush or frontal attack.

When the snows came, the young Highlanders had the additional task of digging out the ditches so enemy parties could not walk across on snowshoes and surprise the fort by a *coup de main*. Clephane even told them how to do it, instructing the young soldiers "to make it up in great Balls and Therewith fill up ye Hollows without the Gate near the Fort." Clephane also ordered "As Often as new Snow falls, and where it holds up, the Serjeants are to turn out some of the men of every Company to Clear the Roof of their Barracks."

Everyday tasks sometimes included the soldier's former trade and occupation. Private Robert Kirkwood of the 42nd Foot, while with his company at Pensacola, FL, in 1766, was employed to mend water casks, "being a cooper by trade." Other important tradesmen were former bakers, tanners, tailors, and saddlers. For any sizable campaign in the wilderness, all armies had to be self-sufficient in skilled laborers, whether regular soldiers, provincials, or hired civilians. The Highland regiments, like others, were liable to be canvassed during siege operations, bateaux building, and fort construction tasks for carpenters, shipwrights, stone masons, brick layers, and wheelwrights. Several Highlanders of the Black Watch, especially those from the western Isles, were re-roled as sailors of the respective sloops launched on Lake Champlain in the 1759 campaign and again for the 1760 campaign on Lake Ontario. Every company had its own tailors supplemented by women acting as seamstresses, as well as a regimental armorer to look after the weapons.

 CHAPLAIN AND WOUNDED AT PLAINS OF ABRAHAM, 1759

It is late afternoon on September 13, 1759, and the Battle of the Plains of Abraham has been over for four hours. Even the fierce post-battle skirmishing is over and a short truce has been declared to collect wounded. Parties are removing wounded off the main battlefield to the southwest (not shown here).

Within cannon shot of Québec's northern walls and defenses, we see the 26-year-old Presbyterian chaplain of the 78th Foot, the Reverend Robert Macpherson, known to his men in Gaelic as *Caipal Mhor* (The Big Chaplain), comforts a dying man. Macpherson is wearing sober civilian clothes with an Inverness district tartan waistcoat and a gold watch chain with Masonic fob. He also sports his family's backsword on his right hip.

The party of four men coming up the slope towards him are carrying a wounded Fraser officer in one of their plaids, a casualty of the Dauphine gun battery visible to the left of the city ramparts. Three of the four men are Highlanders, the fourth man, a hatless member of the Compagnies Franches de la Marine, a colonial prisoner dragooned into service. The vista beyond the smoking city skyline is of the Beauport Shore on the left, while in the center, British warships are anchored in the Québec Basin in front of the Île d'Orléans.

Religious service

A prerequisite of all soldiers enlisting for North America was that they attest in front of a justice of the peace that they were of the Protestant religion, though with the 78th Fraser Highlanders there must have been many cases of a blind eye being turned. Lieutenant Ranald Macdonell of Keppoch, for example, changed his religion in order to get a king's commission, a fact not unnoticed by the clan bard. Keppoch's wounding at the Plains of Abraham was partially seen as God's punishment for his renunciation of the Catholic faith. An excerpt of a song entitled "Raonall Oig Macdonell of Keppoch" translates:

> You were wounded under the belt,
> In your fair, fresh, gentle thigh.
> How it grieves me, that you were so young,
> And that you were won over by love of money
> But that is not surprising, as many worthy men
> Have abandoned their homeland and become turn-coats.

Most young Highland soldiers of the 42nd and 77th Foot had been raised in the Presbyterian faith like William Munro of the 77th, who thought Catholic Ireland to be a godless place. He wrote to his father: "I have not any news to send, but that Country that we are in is very wicked, and the Lord's Day is a day of Feasting, of Drinking, of Dancing and Quarreling, and is Evil Affected to the Government, for the most part of them is Romans, and every night some of them is killing one another."

All three Highland regiments that came to North America during the French-Indian War were blessed with good Presbyterian ministers who were the acknowledged keepers of the regiment's morality and founts of spiritual comfort. The Black Watch had sterling ministers from the day of its raising, and, as such, set a high standard for all Highland regiments that followed. The Reverend James Stewart would die at the Siege of Havana, 1762, ministering to his flock. The two younger Highland regiments raised for service in 1757 also had outstanding chaplains who served with them for the entirety of the war, thus providing continuity and stability for those regiments until they were disbanded.

The 26-year-old chaplain of the 78th Foot was the Reverend Robert Macpherson, known affectionately to his men as the *Caipal Mhor* ("Big Chaplain") because of his towering physique. Macpherson was not shy of soldiering alongside his men and he ensured that "their religious discipline was strictly attended to ... and was indefatigable in the discharge of his clerical duties," so much so, that "the men of the regiment were always anxious to conceal their misdemeanors from the *Caipal Mhor*..."

Freemasonry

After the capture of Québec in 1759, the Freemasons of six regimental field lodges of Wolfe's army decided "that there were so many lodges in the

Two of the three Highland regiments, the 42nd and the 78th, had their own traveling Masonic Lodges, which would operate whenever the regiments were in static garrisons. This master mason's certificate is issued by Lodge 192 of the Grand Lodge of Ireland operating in the 1st Battalion, Black Watch, then in garrison at Montréal, Canada. The five Masonic officers on this 1761 certificate, all sergeants, died of disease the following year at the siege of Havana. (Collection of V.W. Bro. G. W. Bain of Sunderland, with permission of the Grand Lodge of Freemasons of Ireland)

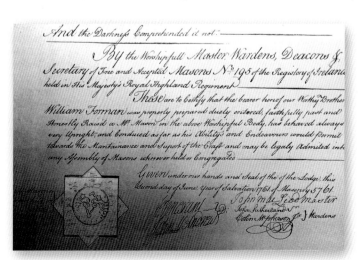

Québec garrison" that they should form themselves into a Grand Lodge and elect a Grandmaster. Sergeant James Thompson was a Freemason, as were many other Highlanders. He knew Reverend Robert Macpherson very well, for after the conquest of New France in 1760 Macpherson, a Freemason himself, served as chaplain to the Québec Select Lodge composed of officers serving in the various regiments then in garrison. Lieutenant Colonel Simon Fraser, Thompson's commanding officer, would be elected Grandmaster of the province of Québec in the summer of 1760 and one of the Grand Lodge's first orders of business was to collect monies for the widows and orphans of fellow Masons killed in battle. Québec Freemasons also provided charitable funds to help the bombed-out inhabitants of the city they now garrisoned as an occupying force.

The Lodge of the 42nd Foot, No.195 of the Grand Lodge of Ireland, had been operating in the Black Watch since 1749. A surviving Master Mason's certificate from their stay in Montréal over the winter of 1760–61 shows the lodge was active in admitting new Freemasons during their stay in North America. Masonic historians concur that it was the traveling lodges of the British Army that helped spread Freemasonry to the colonial units serving alongside them and eventually suffused the whole of colonial administration, society, and culture.

Off-duty pastimes

During James Thompson's stay in the Mohawk Valley during the winter of 1758/59, the majority of the regiment garrisoning Schenectady and its environs enjoyed weekly dances or "frolics, skating, and sleaing parties." One highlight of the winter, reflecting the Highlander's innate competitive nature, was a contest to establish the champion swordsman of the regiment.

Certainly, playing cards and dicing for money topped the list of favorite off-duty pastimes for soldiers shut up in frontier garrisons, especially on the rare occasions they were actually paid. At Fort Stanwix during the winter of 1758/59, Major Clephane was disturbed to learn "that their's [sic] a Great deal of Gaming among the Men both in the Barracks and the Guard Room by which there is a Good Deal of Money Loss'd & Gaind." He strictly forbade such gambling practices and told the sergeants and corporals to clamp down or be "Sivirly Punished" and put under arrest themselves.

Highlanders also liked working with their hands and many carved Celtic designs on their dirk handles or engraved their powder horns with intricate scrimshaw designs. Others less talented enjoyed helping the local inhabitants, with whom they might be billeted. For example, after the fall of New France in 1760, the 78th Foot found itself spread out and garrisoning the many farming communities along the St Lawrence River. Many Highlanders enjoyed helping bring in the harvest and performing simple routine chores on the farms where they were billeted. Those with trades were allowed to work in the city with the permission of their company commanders (and, no doubt, a cut of their earnings). Many secretly married Catholic French-Canadians and would willingly stay behind after the regiment was disbanded.

Food and diet

Highland soldiers were not partial to pork, as many army officers were quick to note. During the raising of the 77th and 78th Foot in Scotland in 1757, the Highland recruits from both battalions billeted in and around Inverness refused to eat the government-issue bacon provided, and tons of it were left to

Playing cards and dicing were two of the favorite off-duty pastimes for soldiers in frontier garrisons, especially on the rare occasions they were actually paid. At Fort Stanwix in 1758–59, gaming in the 78th barracks and guard room got so bad that the Highlanders' commandant had strictly to forbid gambling, and threatened severe punishment and demotion for any NCOs failing to enforce the order. (Tim Todish)

rot at Fort George. In 1759, that dislike manifested itself again with the 2nd Battalion of the 42nd Foot on their summer march to the western end of the Mohawk River Valley to assist with the building of the Fort Oswego on Lake Ontario. Lieutenant John Grant recalled that it was on this march that his young soldiers learned the first of many important lessons while campaigning in the North American wilderness:

Highlanders have a great antipathy to Pork and it was the provision issued to the regts for their march ... but as the soldiers had plenty of money and could get bread butter cheese to purchase at the towns they threw [the pork] away. When they entered the wilderness the provisions were again thrown away, tho' they was warned not to do so, but ignorant of the country they thought that they could still find other foods, [but] to their consternation however the halt was made at night in an uncultivated spot where nothing could be got, they were ashamed to murmur but, next day when the halt was made for breakfast they could no longer hold out and sent a deputation to the Major telling him the circumstances. He said he was sorry for it, but he could issue nothing. There was a general gloom, but luckily it remembered a days provisions had not been issued some previous period.

To the superstitious Highlander, to die far away from one's kith and kin was a terrifying prospect, especially when one of the most damning curses in the Gaelic language was "May you be forgotten forever." Here two Highlanders of the 77th (Montgomery's) remember a fallen comrade in his North American grave "far away from hame" in a modern painting by Robert Griffing. (Robert Griffing & Paramount Press)

Lieutenant Grant recorded that this wilderness breakfast was long remembered and that there was "not a morsel of pork but was cherished with as much care as it had been before regarded with disgust."

The standard weekly issue in North America for all soldiers was known as "Seven rations" and was "seven pounds of beef, or, in lieu thereof, four pounds of pork, which is thought to be equivalent; seven pounds of biscuit bread [hardtack] or the same weight of flour; six ounces of butter, three pints of pease, half a pound of rice." The Highland regiments were happy to accept oatmeal instead of peas or rice so they could make their beloved "porritch."

As the Highlanders were typically billeted together four to six men per tent or hut, the rations were pooled and either a designated cook or one of the company women would have prepared the daily meals. If the Highlanders were billeted with families, such as the 42nd were in Schenectady, NY, during their

 PRIVATE OF THE 42ND FOOT, C. 1756
This private is wearing full Highland dress: (from the top down), a blue bonnet with black bear fur cockade; a white shirt under a short Highland-pattern coat with no lapels; the kilted full plaid known as a *feileadh mór*, buttoned or pinned to the left shoulder. In front, suspended from a waist belt is: a Highland dirk (personal property); a cartouche box for holding his ball cartridges and inscribed with the royal cipher, GR; and, a small sporran or purse (private property). Slung under his right armpit is a traditional Scottish powder horn (personal property) and the all-metal Highland pistol (issue) slung under the left armpit on a thin separate strap. Suspended on a black sword baldric is an army issue backsword. The sword has a Drury-pattern hilt while the dirk is decorated with Celtic carvings. He wears red-and-white diced hose held up with red garters, and on his feet, black shoes with silver buckles. The contents of his haversack are illustrated and include a wooden bowl, a pewter plate, a Highland bone knife, horn porridge spoons, quaich cup, two checkered shirts, a pair of leather gillies, a clasp bible, and a hand-painted Masonic lambskin apron. The contents of his sporran included a money pouch, a pipe with tobacco, flints, fishing gear, musket-cleaning kit, and cards.

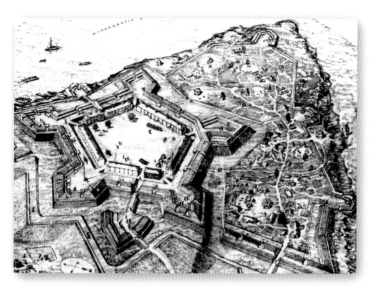

A detail from a reconstructed bird's-eye-view of Fort Pitt c.1764 by Charles Stotz, showing the extensive gardens and fields located outside of the fort used to grow fresh vegetables and corn for the men and hay for the livestock. (Historical Society of Western Pennsylvania, Pittsburgh)

first winter in America, or like the 78th Foot in Connecticut during the winter of 1757/58, the men usually handed their rations over to their hosts, who could then trade with other inhabitants for a more varied and complex diet. In Stratford, CT, James Thompson found himself snugly billeted well in time for Yule and Hogmanay, crowing that he "had the very good luck to get into a very good house own'd by one Thomas Ivers, a ropemaker, where I sat at as well a furnish'd table as my Colonel and as good wine and plenty of it... I lived here like a fighting cock, without it costing me a Copper."

In order to balance the men's diet while stationed at isolated forts such as the Fort Pitt or Fort Stanwix, where scurvy was likely to break out before spring due to a lack of fresh vegetables and an over-dependence on salted meat during the winter, garrison gardens were established so that men and officers alike could grow fresh vegetables such as broccoli, watermelons, cabbage, lettuce, peas, carrots, potatoes, asparagus, squash, and corn. Lieutenant Colonel John Reid, arriving at the Forks of the Ohio in the summer of 1764, reported to his superiors that the fort's commander had kept his Black Watch soldiers busy in the fall and spring and that the:

Gardens are extensive and full of vegetables, which will be more than sufficient to supply the Garrison during the Winter. There are fields of Indian Corn which by computation yield about 400 Bushells; and there is a stack of Spelts and Rye secured below the Shade within the Fort. I have given some directions to have some Hay made, & the Mowers are now at Work: they tell me there is grass enough within a mile of the Fort to make Seven or Eight Cart loads.

Garrisons shut up for the winter would eagerly await the spring "and the grass and weeds to show their heads." One Scottish officer noted that as the snow melted "we are regaled with the root Dandelion, whose leaves make a good salad, and are equal to endives; or, if boiled, eat as well as spinage [sic]." He pronounced this weed "to be highly acceptable to men who have been strangers to every kind of vegetable for several months past."

The more accomplished stalkers and fishermen amongst the Highlanders were always keen to supplement their dreary issue of salted meat and oatmeal with whatever Mother Nature had to offer. James Murray with the 42nd Foot at Lake George wrote his brother in 1758 that "the lake abounds in fine trout the meat of which is red pearch [sic], suckers and several other sorts of fish." Yet every trip away from the safety of camp or garrison was rife with danger, as Indian scalping parties lurked in the woods waiting for just this type of inevitable excursion.

When Capt James Stirling's company of the 42nd Foot traveled down the Ohio from Fort Pitt on their way to take possession of French forts in the Illinois country in 1765, his Highland soldiers observed there were buffalo "as plenty as our black cattle in Europe, the Deer as numerous as our Sheep, and wild Turkeys in as much abundance as our poultry." They "had a good pastime in killing the Buffaloes, which were then in their prime." Most were of the opinion that buffalo was "really most delicious eating. In short, the whole carcase for the purpose of soup-making ... preferable to any of our beef."

A Black Watch officer and the Highlanders of his light infantry detachment deemed his men were better off than the companies assigned to the siege lines at Havana in 1762, for they could scavenge the Cuban countryside. John Grant recalled pillaging the "thickly cultivated gardens for the use of the town" as well as taking numerous cattle in an almost wild state grazing in the fields.

The British Army in North America quickly realized the important link between a soldier's diet and his ability to withstand disease. Perhaps the most common and persistent affliction was scurvy, popularly believed to be the curse and scourge of the Royal Navy in the 18th century. Soldiers in North American winter quarters located far from cities or towns, however, were the most susceptible, having no recourse to fresh vegetables or meat. A diet solely of salt pork, hard biscuit, and rum was almost guaranteed to cause an outbreak of scurvy and one Scot in garrison at Québec in 1760 noted that "it made a dreadful havock amongst us."

James Wolfe, prior to the 1758 Louisburg expedition at Halifax, voiced his concern about the effects the disease had on the fielding of a healthy and efficient assault force: "Some the regiments of this army have 3 or 400 men eaten up with scurvy. The army is undone and ruined by the constant use of salt meat and rum." He predicted dire results if the afflicted soldiers were "wounded or hurt by any accidents," claiming they ran "a great risk of their lives from the corrupted state of their blood."

A preventative measure for scurvy was the issue of "spruce beer" which according to John Knox was:

> an excellent antiscorbutic ... made from the tops and branches of the Spruce-tree, boiled for three hours, then strained into casks, with a certain quantity of molasses; and as soon as it is cold, it is fit for use. When we were incamped at Halifax, the allowance was two quarts a day to each man, or three and a half gallons per week...

Any time troops were assembled and loaded aboard ships in close quarters, the risk of disease ran high and preventative measures were in order. At Halifax in 1758, commanding officers were consistently instructed to ensure "those on board [were] kept extremely clean in their ships, carried frequently on shore and all possible means used to preserve them in health and vigour."

During the 1762 Havana siege, poor water, coupled with the extreme heat, brought on sickness at an alarming rate. One private recalled: "The fatigues on shore were excessive, the bad water brought on disorders, which were mortal, you would see the men's tongues hanging out parch'd like a mad dogs, a dollar was frequently given for a quart of water..." Some men, not trusting the water, resorted to alcohol, the result being widespread drunkenness at all hours of the day. Such hard drinking under a tropical sun contributed to spiraling mortality rates. Some 5,366 soldiers were lost at Havana between June and October 1762, representing about 40 percent of the soldiers present. Of these soldiers, just 560 were killed in action or died of wounds. The remainder, 4,708, succumbed to disease.

In military encampments or fort garrisons where large numbers of men, women, and children were cohabiting, camp sanitation became paramount to prevent sickness and disease. Clephane was horrified during the winter of 1758/59 to find his young Highlanders were not using the "necessary houses" or latrines that had been constructed outside the walls of the fort. He was forced to enact a drastic decree to stop unsanitary and unsavory practices:

> If any man is found to Shite or otherwise nasty the Fort he shall be Oblig'd to clean it with his hands, and no Other Instrument Shall be Allowed, as it is a Scandel & Shame that so much Nastiness Should be seen in the Fort Already... Likewise piss potts which are to Stand at the Door of the Barrack's [are] to be Carried out of the Fort and Cleaned every Morning.

Drink

Drink, understandably, was seen as an evil necessity by most commanders. The navy had its daily issue of rum, as did the army in which a gill or quarter pint of Killdevil was issued to each soldier. Commanders could authorize an extra gill of rum in lieu of money for extra duties such as roadbuilding or fort construction under harsh conditions, if they saw fit. In some cases, soldiers were given extra gills on their return from strenuous patrols or successful expeditions. At the siege of Havana in 1762, Col James Grant, formerly of Montgomery's Highlanders, "was appointed to superintend the works. He put it in some more Methods & gave grogg liberally, which had its effects."

On or off duty, Highland regiments were certainly less prone to drunkenness than provincial or regular British regiments. One provincial observed in a letter to the *Pennsylvania Gazette* that the men of the 42nd Foot garrisoning Fort Edward in 1756 were not like the other troops at Fort Edward, who "lie stinking in their tents," but were "a Sett of fine Men, quiet and sober." Needless to say, enterprising soldiers could always find drink somewhere and for soldiers cooped up in the isolated garrison forts such as Edward, Crown Point, and Pitt, however, there was little to do in the off-duty hours but eat, sleep, gamble, and drink. At Fort Stanwix in 1759, Major Clephane wrote that drunkenness had become a serious problem for his 400-man garrison as the men began "to debauch themselves by Drinking a Great Deal too much Pernicious & hurtful ... New England Rum."

Drink also began to erode discipline. An entry in Fort Orders for November 17, 1758, reads:

> Several Complaints having been Made that a good deal of his Majesty's stores particularly Rum have been stole, even tho' under the care and Eye of a sentry, major Clephane therefore orders to tell the men that if any such thing happen after this, and it may be proved the sentry does it himself, or Connives at any other Doing it; all Consern'd will be Equally punish'd to the Outmost rigour of the Law; As it is a scandle and a shame that such things Should happen amongst Regular Troops.

Strictures against the sale of alcohol were usually relaxed after a successful campaign or when regiments went into winter quarters. While heavy drinking could be a killer in hot or cold climates, it was also one of the principal causes of army crime. British historian Stephen Brumwell in *Redcoats*, his excellent study of the British soldier in North America, has remarked "it is unusual to find a court case in which alcohol [did] not play some part." Absence without leave, insolence, violence against superiors, theft, and murder were common outcomes of too much drink and dealt with accordingly by general courts-martial.

This contemporary water color by Lieutenant Thomas Davies of the Royal Artillery is a vista showing Crown Point on Lake Champlain – the new British fort under construction starts to take shape. The extensive tent lines and huts house BrigGen William Haviland's army poised to move against Montréal. (Library of Congress).

Crime and punishment

If we are to believe David Stewart of Garth's stereotype of the 18th-century Highland soldier, they were never drunk, never cold, never afraid, never homesick, never mutinous, and never deserted. While this may have been the case before the outbreak of the Seven Years' War, which found his own regiment, the 42nd Foot, enjoying the idyllic fruits of peace in quiet Irish cantonments after the War of Austrian Succession (1743–48), this high moral conduct certainly cannot be ascribed to the lowly privates of the overnight Highland battalions raised in 1757 for service in North America, the 77th and 78th Foot.

"Although it is true that Highlanders feature far less frequently in the General Courts Martial records than miscreants from [English] battalions," says Stephen Brumwell, "it would be wrong to go to the other extreme and suggest their ranks were filled with plaster saints." To do so based on the official records and courts-martial of the day, is a naïve perspective – particularly given the often lawless nature of traditional Highland society. It also overlooks the fact that these regiments had their own internal mechanisms for punishing petty crimes and misdemeanors, sometimes brutally.

For example, a young private soldier of the 2nd/42nd Foot was awarded 999 lashes for leaving his sentry post without permission at Albany, NY, in 1760. The truth be told, Highlanders, including their officers, during the Seven Years' War would be found guilty of serious crimes ranging from murder and assault, to desertion, extortion, and rape. During the Black Watch's first winter in North America, two men deserted from the Schenectady garrison. The entire battalion turned out to look for them, the honor of the regiment at stake. The miscreants were quickly captured, court-martialed and shot.

They would not be the last, either. Numerous soldiers of the 77th Foot would desert in South Carolina to start a new life amongst a sympathetic populace, many of them their own countrymen.

While the Highlanders were encamped outside Charles Town after their return from their 1760 expedition against the Cherokees, 16 of their number deserted, Col Montgomery informing MajGen Amherst that the culprits from his regiment were "some of the best men, most of them tradesmen who were of great use." He posted a reward of £100 (Carolina currency) for every deserter apprehended and a £50 reward to anyone providing information leading to a capture. "A description of them has been left" he wrote, "but we were not able to get one of them."

Punishment in the British Army was quick and severe, the lash or cat o' nine tails being the most common chastisement of the common soldier and the origin of the standard provincial epithet normally thrown their way – "Bloodybacks." Yet cases of Highlanders being flogged are few and far between in general and regimental orders.

Women and children

The majority of Highlanders who came to North America during the French-Indian War were young, unmarried men, including their officers. The married men tended to be the sergeants and corporals that had seen long service, especially the ones who had transferred from the other British regiments into the new 77th and 78th Regiments of Foot. The Highland regiments, like other line regiments of the day, were authorized an establishment of six women per company, who were expected to perform myriad chores from cooking and sewing to nursing and laundering.

Captain Edward Wells of the Connecticut Provincials noted with great interest the arrival of the Black Watch at Fort Edward in September 1756: "A regm't of Highlanders came in with Drums, trumpets and bagpipes going, sounding sweetly, women and children with them." The manifests of the eight transports that carried Fraser's Highlanders from Halifax to New York in 1757 reveal that that regiment had 110 women and 29 children on strength, as well as 1,135 all ranks.

Many wives became sutlers, enterprising tradesfolk who acted as money-changers, or sold small luxury items not provided by the army. Fiercely independent and aggressive, they sometimes incurred the wrath of commanders by selling too much liquor or flouting camp discipline. The 42nd Highlanders' orders for May 17, 1759, in Albany stated that "all the petit Sutlers tents in the rear or any other whereabout the Regt" were to be "struck immediately and if any woman whatsoever pretends to pitch tent about after this, near the regt, the Qr. Mr. is to order it to be struck and burnt directly."

ON CAMPAIGN

Death is the least misfortune.
– Colonel Henri Bouquet

On the topic of waging war in the wilderness of the North America, a Swiss officer astutely observed that, before one could close with one's enemy and defeat him, a soldier had first to contend with the weather and terrain:

> In an American campaign everything is terrible; the face of the country, the climate, the enemy. There is no refreshment for the healthy, nor relief for the sick. A vast inhospitable desert, unsafe and treacherous, surrounds them, where victories are not decisive, but defeats are ruinous; and simple death is the least misfortune, which can happen to them. This forms a service truly critical, in which all the firmness of the body and mind is put to the severest trial; and all the exertions of courage and address are called out.

Climate, wildlife, terrain – all provided their own particular dangers for the unprepared or inattentive soldier. The Highland soldier, however, came with more preparation for an inhospitable environment than most.

Weather

A Highlander was no stranger to snowstorms and icy weather, but it was at Québec where the Fraser Highlanders would be most severely tested by sub-zero weather, which would force them to don woolen breeches and leggings

under their kilts to prevent frostbite. All of Wolfe's victorious army forced to winter in that bombed-out city, where they served on sentry duty, wood-cutting parties, or combat patrols, quickly discovered that their army issue clothing was ill-suited to withstand the rigors of the North American climate.

Lieutenant Malcolm Fraser of the 78th Foot wrote in his journal of how his Highlanders suffered from simple everyday tasks such as mounting guard or going beyond the fortress walls to chop much-needed firewood:

> …the winter is become insupportably cold. The men are notwithstanding oblig'd to drag all the wood used in the Garrison on sledges from St. Foy, about four miles distance. This is very severe duty; the poor fellows do it however with great spirit; 'tho several of them have already lost the use of their fingers and toes by the incredible severity of the frost, and the country people tell us it is not yet at the worst. Some men on sentry have been deprived of speech and sensation in a few minutes, but hitherto, no person has lost his life, as care is taken to relieve them every half-hour or oftener when the weather is very severe.

Fraser would confess that Highland dress was "not at all calculated for this terrible climate," adding that "Colonel Fraser is doing all in his power to provide trousers for [us] and we hope to soon to be on a footing with the other regiments." By January 1760, the 78th Foot was indistinguishable from all the other regiments, "the weather such that [we] are obliged to have all

A view of Havana from inside its natural harbor looking out. Highlanders besieged and assaulted the formidable fortress called the Moro Castle seen on the heights to the right of the entrance after mines were fired by the Royal Engineers, creating a hole in the walls. (Courtesy, Library of Congress)

covered but [our] eyes, and nothing but the last necessity obliged any man to go out of doors." Captured French blankets in the city stores were issued to all regiments and cut up to provide woolen socks and mittens for the men. With temperatures consistently registering at -20°F (without wind-chill factored in), officers and men cared little about their personal appearance.

To the south in New York colony, the 42nd Foot's officers allowed leggings to be worn with the full-belted plaid. A November 6, 1759 orderly book entry at Crown Point reveals: "The Non-Commissioned Officers & men will be allowed until further orders to do duty in there Kilt over their leggans." When both battalions went into winter quarters one of their first priorities was to ensure that all new clothing was "to be fitted and the waistcoats made as fast as possible that the men may be warmly clad during the severity of the Winter, and it is recommended to the Commanding Officers that every man has a warm cloth cap made."

On the other extreme was the debilitating heat of the tropics, and many Highlanders in Martinique and Cuba for the 1762 Caribbean campaigns preferred night operations to avoid the sweltering heat of the cane fields and jungles by day. The soldiers of the "American Army" seemed to have fared slightly better than the newly arrived battalions from Europe, who were still dressed for fighting a conventional war. Commanding officers of these European units had to be instructed "to order the Lining ... riped [sic] out of the Mens Cloaths, the Lapels to be taken off and Skirts cut Short." Heat exhaustion, sunstroke, and dehydration weakened the men to such a state that yellow fever, malaria, and dysentery became rampant. Mortality rates by disease surpassed those of men killed in action by six to one.

The Highlanders of the 2nd Battalion of Royal Highlanders that came to North America via the Caribbean in 1757 certainly found the transition to be drastic to say the least. When they disembarked from boats at Albany many of their comrades were left there, still weakened from their tropical fevers. They then marched and boated along the Mohawk Valley on their way to Oswego on Lake Ontario, encountering dark and endless woods stretching out before them, filled with wolves, Indians, and other unforeseen dangers which could, and did, strike without warning. As they marched across the Great Carrying Place near present-day Rome, NY, one Highlander recorded how:

> ...a most terrible storm overtook us – rain, wind, thunder and lightening – the scene was terrific, the boldest trembled – trees falling in every direction, deluge of rain, and as we were afraid of attack from the Indians, we took off our bonnets to protect our pieces, and thus bareheaded we bore the pelting of the pitiless storm, the water running out of our shoes, some of our men were hurt and the adjutant was nearly killed by the falling of a tree.

Wildlife

Not only could the climate be disagreeable and terrifying. By the end of August, John Grant and his Highlanders had nearly reached their destination of Oswego and were rowing down Wood Creek. They landed for the night and an officer's picket of 50 men was posted on the river bank "to keep watch for Indians." That night, Grant went down to the river's edge and could not resist "imitating the yelp of a dog" and was instantly rewarded with "a serenade of the Bullfrogs and the Wolves ... as if Pandemonium had broke loose [and] we were almost afraid of them, but as wood was not scarce [we] had roaring fires."

Every step of their journey they had been "daily tormented by mosquitoes," an insect that one Scot confessed to be so troublesome and "inexpressibly teasing" that he had witnessed "many people thrown into fevers by their virulence, and a person's head, face and neck so swelled and inflamed as not to have a feature distinguishable." At Louisburg, the Fraser Highlanders and other regiments were plagued with blood-sucking blackflies and deerflies, causing the men to build large smoky fires in an effort to find some relief.

While at Québec, the Fraser Highlanders found that they had to share the remaining habitable buildings with all sorts of vermin trying to find some warmth during the sub-zero winter. They were explicitly warned to hang up their food, snowshoes, and leather accoutrements so they would not be eaten by "Rotts and meace."

While the Black Watch was encamped at Lake George in upcountry New York, one Highlander noted there was "plenty of beavers [while] on the other side of the lake there is plenty of deer but I have not seen any since I came to this country." There were also snakes to contend with, James Murray claiming that while out on patrol he had "killed rattlesnakes about four feet long and as thick as the small of one's leg." Speaking from personal experience he added:

> When touched they make a great noise with their rattles. Their bite is not so bad as called, for it can be easily cured with oil or salt. They smell exactly like a goat, rather ranker if possible before they are seized but afterwards they have no smell at all. They make the richest and best soup that can be which I eat of and like much.

Highlanders going down the Ohio and Mississippi rivers as far as New Orleans encountered an incredibly rich and diverse profusion of wildlife never seen before in their homeland: buffalo, antelope, prairie dogs, pelicans, giant catfish, and alligators.

Terrain

Terrain could also be unforgiving, and Highland soldiers quickly adopted leggings over their hose to protect them from wear and tear, but also to protect their legs from poison ivy, poison sumac, and brambles when moving through the woods.

In a rugged environment where rivers and lakes were the principal highways through the North American wilderness, whaleboats, such as that in the reconstruction pictured here, along with "battoes" (slightly larger), were essential in moving large numbers of men and materiel of the various armies over long distances. (Private collection)

Highlanders were shocked by the scalped and mutilated victims they encountered in western Pennsylvania and other theaters of war. Private Robert Kirkwood wrote indignantly: "Whoever was so unhappy as to fall into the hands of these inhuman wretches, was either scalped and burnt or otherways barbarously used." (Dover Pictorial Archives)

Snow meant that isolated forts in the wilderness were cut off from civilization and any real contact with the outside world. Numerous men drowned traversing rotten ice in spring. When Highlanders at Fort Stanwix in early 1759 were starting to sicken at an alarming rate with scurvy, Major Clephane wrote of the extreme difficulty in getting reinforcements upcountry:

> The Officers who came here with the detachment of forty men sent here by Colonel Fraser to relieve our sickly men made report to me that it was with the utmost difficulty they got to us here as the River and creeks are all so swelled by the late thaw; the detachment brought two sleas with them in order to assist our sick men in going down the country to Schenectady, but as they were oblidg'd to cause the horses and sleas swim the creeks, two of their horses and one slea was carried away, and the two horses drowned. As the roads and the creeks are so bad, I have only sent down the officers who came hence from Fort Herkemer [with] 25 of our best sick men who our surgeon thinks may be able to make it out.

Death by drowning was a common occurrence, given the constant boat service required to ferry supplies up and down the lakes and rivers. Sudden thunderstorms on any of the Great Lakes meant certain death for men in small whaleboats or bateaus. Private Kirkwood of the 77th warned that on Lake Erie, "you meet with a long range of highlands, which is very dangerous in passing, for if a storm should arise, your boats will inevitably be dashed to pieces and every soul lost." Two years after Kirkwood's successful passage of this stretch, a sudden November storm devastated a British fleet of bateaux carrying 600 troops and much needed supplies from Niagara to Detroit. Boats were shattered like matchwood, 70 men drowned, and vast quantities of ammunition and provisions were lost. Equally dangerous was the practice of running rapids to avoid portaging, a long laborious process of unloading boats and carrying them and their cargoes manually overland until a quieter stretch of water was reached.

Scalping and torture

The few journals and memoirs of Highlanders that survive today from the French-Indian War are full of repugnance for the Indian (and colonial) practice of scalping. Soldiers of the Black Watch first encountered it in the fall of 1756 when some of their comrades were killed and mutilated. "They say the Highlanders are so set upon going against the Enemy, that their Officers were obliged to take away their Broadswords, and put them in the Stores," claimed a provincial officer, adding that the Highlanders "highly resent the cruel Usage the Indians have given some of their Friends."

When the Fraser Highlanders first went into action at the siege of Québec in 1759, their innocence and naïveté was shattered by "the wrecked heads" (as one Gaelic poet put it) of mates killed fighting against Huron, Abneki, and Iroquois warriors that lurked on the perimeters of their encampments. Eighteen-year-old Malcolm Fraser observed "several dead bodies on the road, not far from our Camp; they were all scalped and mangled in a shocking manner. I dare say no human creature but an Indian or Canadian could be guilty of such inhumanity as to insult a dead body."

That the Highlanders had not adopted the retaliatory measures taken by some other British regiments against their Indian adversaries (thus perpetuating the atrocities) is proven by a tongue-in-cheek newspaper report that appeared in a New York paper after Louisburg the previous year: "About 100 Frenchmen were made prisoners immediately after landing, and a great many Indians killed, amongst whom, it is said, their Chief; and that several of the Savages were taken alive by the Highlanders, whose Heads they chopped off immediately, not being acquainted with the Method of Scalping." The editor makes a not so subtle suggestion that the Indians' savage ways would soon compel the Highlanders to take up this barbaric custom, although in fact this did not happen.

As the 1759 siege at Québec dragged on through the summer and irregular warfare was stepped up, Gen Wolfe officially authorized the scalping of Indians, or "Canadians dressed as Indians," and offered a bounty of £5 for every Indian scalp brought in. In a skirmish on August 23, 1759, a number of Canadians painted and dressed as Indians were taken prisoner by the Highlanders. According to one of their own officers, these captives were then "butchered in a most inhuman and cruel manner" by a captain from another regiment and some rangers.

One of the most feared aspects of war on the frontier for soldiers and civilians alike was the possibility of being taken captive by Indians. Here in a painting by Robert Griffing entitled *He Befriended Me Greatly*, Shawnee Indians capture Robert Kirkwood of Montgomery's Highlanders during Grant's Raid at Fort Duquesne in August 1758. His harrowing account was preserved in a small obscure book entitled *The Memoirs and Adventures of Robert Kirk; Late of the Royal Highland Regiment*, published in Limerick, Ireland, 1775. (Robert Griffing and Paramount Press)

Soldiers such as Private Robert Kirkwood of Montgomery's Highlanders saw friends scalped and tortured before his very eyes, an experience that no doubt brutalized the young Scot and steeled him for future combat in the Americas. At Fort Duquesne, 1758, after being taken prisoner by the Shawnee, he watched as friends were "scourg'd, and tortur'd the entire day." Kirkwood escaped the ordeal as his captor "befriended him greatly" and adopted him into the tribe to replace a fallen warrior.

At the Battle of Sillery outside Québec in April 1760, the last land battle fought in North America during the French-Indian War, the enemy's penchant for scalping was unabated. Many wounded and sick Highlanders and men of the other regiments "Faint and intirely [sic] unable for a precipitate flight" when the order came to retreat, fell victim to the tomahawk and scalping knife. Major Patrick Mackellar, the Scottish chief engineer, despite being seriously wounded, was one of the lucky few to escape the battle's aftermath and bitterly remembered that the "dead, all the wounded men and several of the wounded officers who could not get off the field was, as usual, every one Scalped for the entertainment of the Conqueror."

Medical services

Highland soldiers, if wounded in set-piece battles, could expect some form of rudimentary care from the primitive medical system the 18th-century British Army had in place. Each regiment had a surgeon who was commissioned and accorded officer status by virtue of his appointment and social standing. Usually, he held a medical degree from a recognized university of the day and was assisted by a warranted surgeon's mate, regimental orderlies (usually musicians), and those regimental women who were experienced nurses.

Typically, each regiment would establish its own hospital in a dwelling or a tent when encamped, which was then run by the surgeon's mate and his orderlies. Each morning, sick or injured soldiers would attend the daily "sick parade," with only medical cases beyond the mate's scope and expertise being referred to the doctor.

78TH FOOT GRENADIERS, BATTLE OF SILLERY, QUÉBEC, 1760

This plate depicts the morning action on the firing line at the Battle of Sillery, April 28, 1760, outside Québec City on the western edge of Plains of Abraham. Here we see the left flank of the 78th Foot's grenadier company, three hours into the battle. Many dead and wounded litter the blood-stained snow and the Highlanders are low on ammunition and taking heavy casualties standing in the open. They are easy targets for French marksmen situated on the edge of the Sillery Woods to their right front, a mere 20 yards away.

It is a critical moment. The grenadier company is on the verge of collapse and their last officer has gone down. With bayonets fixed, they are at the carry awaiting the command to reload. Sergeant James Thompson has scrambled forward over the ground littered with dead and wounded and is attempting to keep the line steady and intact. "It was my lot to act as covering sergeant to Captain Fraser," he recalled, but moved forward when his company commander Capt Alexander Fraser of Culduthel "received a shot in the temple and, as not an inch of ground was to be lost, I had to move up into line which I could not do without resting one foot on his body."

About ten minutes later the British artillery pieces, which had been sited between the stretched British battalions and had been keeping the more numerous French force at bay by firing grape, fell silent, one by one. The French quickly advanced and collapsed the left flank of the small, sickly British army. Thompson and his men were ordered to fall back to the city over a mile away, the dead and wounded being left where they fell. Many of the grenadiers in Thompson's company who had come out of the hospital to fight were still sick with scurvy and too weak to make the return journey. They quickly fell victim to the scalping knives, or if they were lucky, were taken prisoner by the French.

Located approximately half a mile to the north outside Québec City, this hospital was filled to overflowing with French and British wounded after the Battle of the Plains of Abraham, 1759. Run by the Augustinian order, this remarkable facility and its trained nursing sisters probably saved many wounded men's lives on both sides. (Courtesy, David M. Stewart Museum Library)

Field hospitals, with special officers attached to them, were established in time of war to take the sick and wounded overflow from the regimental hospitals. The General Hospital established at Albany early on in the French-Indian War is a good example, and French hospitals captured at Québec were put into good use in 1759. Barracks in New York, Elizabethtown, and Amboy were converted into hospitals in 1762 in an attempt to treat the huge numbers of fever-ridden men coming back from the Caribbean operations. When these became full and hospital beds were at a premium, some sick and wounded Highlanders found themselves billeted with the inhabitants of the colony in which their regiment was campaigning.

Highlanders, like other British regulars, were discharged when seriously wounded or injured beyond 100 percent recovery. Some who were lucky could reenlist in invalid companies, which traditionally garrisoned harbor defenses in Britain. Others, if fortunate enough to have had more than 20 years' service before being incapacitated, could apply to the Royal Hospitals at Chelsea in London or Kilmainham in Dublin as potential pensioners. The majority, however, became beggars on the streets of the cities, visible reminders of Britain's overseas wars.

THE EXPERIENCE OF BATTLE

The battles and sieges of James Thompson

At 4 o'clock on the morning of June 8, 1758, the first wave of boats containing "the four Eldest Company of Grenadiers" and one of the most junior units in the entire British army – 100 Highland grenadiers of the 78th Foot under the command of Capt Charles Baillie – set off for the large curving sandy beach at Coromandière Cove, some 4 miles to the west of the fortress port of Louisburg. British strategy called for Louisburg's capture in 1759 before British forces could safely sail up the St Lawrence and place the capital of Québec under siege. Failure to do so would leave an enemy port behind them and astride their critical lines of resupply and reinforcement.

Each grenadier company was crammed into large custom-built landing craft commonly referred to as "flat-bottomed boats." There had been no room for the normal complement of 18 sailors to man the oars of the large shallow-drafted craft, so now they were being towed by the boats of the fleet through a heavy swell.

A second wave of ships' boats followed closely behind in the pewter-gray dawn. Those without flint capes had wrapped their firelock mechanisms with rags to keep their powder pans dry, for all men were soon wet in the flying spray. These were the 550 "chosen men" of Major George Scott's Provisional Battalion of Light Infantry. One fifth of them were handpicked Highlanders from the three Additional Companies of the 78th Foot who had joined their regiment in Connecticut in April, fresh from the Highlands. The rest of the 78th Foot, commanded by Simon Fraser, were in the third wave with the remaining grenadier companies of the army. All three waves comprised the assault force under command of the mercurial and tempestuous James Wolfe, colonel of the 67th Foot and "Brigadier in America."

James Thompson and the Fraser Highlanders were going into action for the first time and he remembers the beach they approached as being strangely silent, except for the ever-present crash of the North Atlantic surf. When the leading boats were a mere 30 yards from the beach, swathes of camouflage, which had been cunningly placed to hide French entrenchments and gun batteries, were suddenly pushed forward or pulled aside by their occupants. Seconds later, the entire shoreline erupted with a blaze of fire from 6pdr, 9pdr, and 24pdr guns. Swivel guns stuffed with nails, glass, and chewed bullets spewed forth their deadly contents. The aimed musketry of 1,200 men of the Artois regiment, Acadian militia, and the French Navy added to the din, rattling up and down the beach like a *feu de joie* (literally "fire of joy," a gun salute) gone crazy.

Major Alexander Murray, 45th Foot, one of the two senior officers commanding the first wave, described it as "a most prodigious fire" that "fell all around us just as if we had taken handfuls of shot and thrown them into the water." One British sergeant standing up in his boat exclaimed: "Who would not go to Hell, to hear such music for half an hour?" then promptly fell dead as his boat was raked from stem to stern by French swivels discharging grape shot. A boat packed with grenadiers of the 15th Foot was smashed by a shot and "sunk, by which one Officer, two sergeants and thirty fine fellows were lost" except for the drummer, who "buoy'd up by his drum" was saved. Even the gallant James Wolfe flinched in the face of such a furious fire.

The first wave of Major George Scott's highly trained light infantry land at a small unguarded cove to the east of the main French beach defenses, causing the defenders to panic and retreat. The Frasers were the next wave ashore and participated in the rout of the French over 6 miles of bog and forest back to the town fortress of Louisburg. (Painting by Steve Noon from Osprey's Warrior 88: *British Light Infantryman of the Seven Years' War* by Ian McCulloch and Tim Todish)

"The French were peppering us with canister shot from a six-gun battery on the heights," recalled Grenadier Sgt James Thompson of the 78th Foot, "while musket balls fired by 24-pounders came whistling about our ears!" The pounding of their own warships providing anti-battery fire to cover the landing, added to the noise and smoke and made "a terrific hullabaloo."

Eventually a French cannonball hit home. It turned Thompson's boat into a charnel house because they "were so closely packed together there was only room for us to stand up except in the back part where the officers and NCOs contrived to sit." A 24pdr solid shot "did a great deal of mischief," cutting a swathe through the dense mass of helpless Highlanders. Thompson felt the actual ball as it "passed under my hams and killed Sgt Mackenzie who was sitting as close to my left as he could squeeze, and it carried away the basket of his broadsword which, along with the shot, passed through Lieutenant Cuthbert, who was on Mackenzie's left, tore his body into shivers, and cut off both legs of one of the two fellows who manned the tiller of the boat, who lost an astonishing quantity of blood, and died with the tiller grasped tightly in his hand."

Wolfe was about to order a withdrawal when he caught sight of a boat of light infantry signaling on the far left of the beach where surf crashed against a rocky headland projecting outwards some 20 yards. He then quickly noticed that two other boats of light infantry had just landed in a tiny sheltered cove to the right of the said headland, out of sight, and hence the line of fire, of the heavily entrenched French positions on the main beach.

The cove (later named Wolfe's Cove) was minuscule, no more than 12 yards across, but the light infantry were ashore, scrambling up a small wooded hill that guarded the right flank of the French position. Among them were Fraser's gentlemen volunteers as well as the light infantry company in their distinctive blue bonnets and philabegs, led by Capt Alexander Cameron of Dungallon.

Wolfe ordered the rest of the flotilla to shift right and take their chances landing at the same spot, which was unmolested by the heavy French fire. More troops scrambled ashore and one of their officers climbed the hill covered with brushwood. "Going a short way" recalled Thompson, the officer found "himself at the edge of the brushwood, and beheld to his great astonishment the French army form'd in their trenches [below him] where he stood." The lieutenant returned and gave orders: "Squads each to Sally out in turn from the Brushwood, and fire at the French, and then return to the rear to reload in order to conceal their numbers."

Parson Robert MacPherson, the *Caipal Mhor* of the 78th Foot, recorded that the first men to get ashore at the cove after the light infantry and Wolfe were 400 to 500 Highlanders of the bonnet companies of the 78th under Col Fraser. The light infantry, Highlanders, and rangers moved down off the hill, and attempted to get in behind the French entrenchments and cut off their escape.

Thompson somewhat gleefully wrote: "The French supposing … they were attacked by a numerous body of our troops betook themselves to their Seraphers and away they ran to the Garrison which was about three miles distance from the trenches they had just quit."

Thompson, veteran of the 78th Foot, would continue to live a charmed life throughout the rest of the war and the next conflict as well – the American Revolution – living to a ripe old age of 97. In 1759 Thompson would fight with his grenadiers at the famous battles of Montmorency and the Plains of Abraham with Wolfe's victorious army. Of the latter battle his recollections were typical of most soldiers: pure unadulterated elation and pride in what they accomplished. "If the French gave themselves quietly up, they had no harm done to them," he remembered, "But Faith! If they tried to outrun a Hielandmon, they stood but a bad chance, for Whash! went the broadsword."

A second emotion in evidence was a sober recollection of the battle's harrowing aftermath:

The casualties lay on the field as thick as a flock of sheep and just as they had fallen, for the main body had been completely routed off the ground and had no opportunity of carrying away their dead and wounded. We killed seventy-two officers [including non-commissioned officers] alone, and it was horrid to see the effect of blood and dust on their white coats.

Among the British casualties was the beloved "Red-haired Corporal" – Gen James Wolfe. Iain Campbell addressed the Highlanders' genuine grief by composing extra verses for his famous song, adroitly weaving the young general forever into the regiment's rich tapestry of great deeds, ensuring that Wolfe became part of their glorious history, always present, and never forgotten:

The flowing blood of our renowned General
Was soaking into the grass
And it was a terrible loss,
Though it is a great tale to tell…

The Fraser Highlanders and other regiments of James Wolfe's army land under the Heights of Abraham west of Québec and climb 300ft to the plains above, where they would fight and win the first set-piece European-style battle fought in North America. (National Archives of Canada)

He asked to be lifted, so that he could see
The battle, while he was in that terrible plight!
He could not see the heroes
As death took away his sight!
They said to him in high spirits,
"We have suddenly won the battlefield,
And the Gaels are among them
Wounding them as they run downhill."
        O Lads make ready....

James Thompson's final battle of the French-Indian War would be a defeat at the hands of Gén Lévis' Franco-Canadian army in April 1760, the small and scurvy-ridden British army retreating after a bloody toe-to-toe battle of three hours' duration outside the walls of Québec. The exhausted and hungry French army promptly encamped outside, but were exposed to the elements and had lost so many officers and the "flower of their army" that they were not able to press home the final assault. The Royal Navy would arrive some weeks later, destroying the French transports and forcing the French to withdraw to Montréal. Thompson and the 78th Foot would participate in the bloodless capture of Montréal and the surrender of New France later that year.

As a military action during the French-Indian War, the Battle of Sillery ranks as a bloodier, more bravely and skillfully fought action than that of September 13, 1759, by Gen Wolfe. The Plains of Abraham however, has continued to hold the public's imagination for time immemorial, rooted in an unshakeable mythology that has grown up and solidified around the daring surprise landing and climbing of the cliffs at the Anse au Foulon and the noble and tragic deaths of Wolfe, and his French opponent, Gén Louis-Josephe de Montcalm.

James Thompson would face one last siege in his military career. As the civilian overseer of the fortifications at Québec in 1775, he would be instrumental in assisting in the successful defense of the city against Gen Richard Montgomery's and Benedict Arnold's American forces in their bold attempt to seize the city. Many former Fraser Highlanders would subsequently join the Royal Highland Emigrants (84th Foot) and soldier once more for king and country in that war. But that is another story.

An engraving of the painting *The Death of General James Wolfe, 1759* completed by Benjamin West in 1770. It clearly shows Lieutenant Colonel Simon Fraser of the 78th Highlanders standing behind a Ranger officer (allegedly Robert Rogers). Historically, Fraser, wounded a month earlier, was not present at the battle, nor present at Wolfe's death. (Library of Congress).

AFTERMATH

Having undergone the most amazing fatigues
– Benjamin Franklin, 1767

Undoubtedly, the exploits of the 42nd (Black Watch), 77th (Montgomery's), and 78th (Fraser's) Highlanders, in some of the most bloody and desperate battles ever fought on the North American continent, were a critical factor in transforming the overall image of Highlanders from Jacobite rebels to imperial heroes in the latter half of the 18th century.

From the windswept crags of Signal Hill in Newfoundland to the Forks of the Ohio in the Pennsylvanian wilderness, and from the Great Lakes and outposts of New France to the torrid cane fields and swamps of the Caribbean isles, young Highlanders soldiered in the New World for the first time, and many of those who survived the horrors stayed or returned later with families to make it their home.

In 1763, with the peace and the reduction of the 77th and 78th Regiments looming, the remains of the 77th and 42nd Highlanders recovering from the siege of Havana on Long Island, NY, were brigaded together under the command of the famous Col Henri Bouquet and sent to the western frontiers to fight one last time. There, an Indian uprising was raging and they found themselves fighting for their lives at an obscure place named Bushy Run in the Pennsylvanian wilderness.

The veteran Highlanders beat off their assailants and won through to relieve the besieged garrison of Fort Pitt at the Forks of the Ohio. Almost immediately after this small, sharp engagement, the 77th were finally disbanded, as were the 78th Foot in Québec. Half of the 160 Highlanders of James Thompson's regiment, who elected to remain behind in North America chose to settle in Québec, while as many as 80 sergeants, corporals, and privates returned to the fertile Mohawk Valley in New York colony to take up land grants and settle there. Soldiers of the 77th settled in Nova Scotia, upstate New York, and the Carolinas.

The remaining Highland regiment, the Black Watch, now reduced to one battalion of 700 men, would spend the rest of its stay in North America manning Fort Pitt, and guarding the line of communications back to Philadelphia. In the summer of 1767, the Royal Highlanders would muster in "The City of Brotherly Love" and board a transport ship to take them back to Ireland after 11 years of hard soldiering in the American wilderness and far-flung Caribbean isles. Benjamin Franklin's laudatory tribute to the regiment in the pages of the *Pennsylvania Gazette*, dated July 30, 1767, could equally apply to the service of its two younger sister battalions – the 77th and 78th Regiments of Foot – while in North America. Franklin praised them for:

> …having undergone most amazing fatigues, made long and frequent marches through an inhospitable country, bearing excessive heat and severe cold with alacrity and cheerfulness, frequently encamping in deep snow, such as those that inhabit the interior parts of this province do not see, and which only those who inhabit the northern parts of Europe can have any idea of, continually exposed in camp, and on their marches, to the alarms of a savage enemy, who, in all their attempts, were forced to fly…

They have our thanks for that decorum in behaviour which they maintained

Overleaf "We gave them our whole fire and rushed out upon them with fixt bayonets." On the first encounter with the attacking Indians at Bushy Run on the afternoon of August 5, 1763, Robert Kirkwood and his fellow Highlanders of the 42nd and 77th Foot gave the enemy cold steel. A detail from Robert Griffing's painting *One Mile to Bushy Run*. (Robert Griffing and Paramount Press)

during their stay in this city, giving an example that the most amiable behaviour in civil life is no way inconsistent with the character of the good soldier; and for their loyalty, fidelity, and orderly behaviour, they have every wish of the people for health, honour, and a pleasant voyage.

G HIGHLANDERS' CHARGE, BUSHY RUN, 1763

During the Pontiac Indian uprising of 1763, Col Henri Bouquet, a Swiss officer, was sent west to relieve Fort Ligonier and Fort Pitt, taking with him with a force of 390 Highlanders, a dozen Royal Americans, as well as a small detachment of Maryland rangers and some Pennsylvanian packhorse drivers. On August 5, 1763, Bouquet's small relief column was attacked and encircled by Ohio Indians at Edge Hill, shown here.

Looking down, we see in the right bottom corner of the plate, the flourbag defensive position (the "keep" on the summit of the convex hill in which the wounded and gunpowder barrels were placed.) Just to the left, the surviving packhorses were tethered in one group and the cattle in another.

The Indians remained at a distance, sniping and using their war cries to dishearten the surrounded force running short of water. Col Bouquet decided on the second day, August 6, to use an old Indian tactic – a feigned retreat – to lure the Indians in as close as possible. He ordered the 77th and 42nd light companies, as well as their grenadiers, to withdraw precipitously from the front perimeter as if retreating in fear, then to quickly exit at the southern end of the fortified hill which the Indians had left open and regroup there in the dead ground as a mobile strike force.

In the left bottom quarter we thus see the light infantry and grenadier companies of the Highlanders launching their surprise counterattack and successfully rolling up the right flank of the massed Indians, who have taken the bait and have closed in for the kill. In the right top quarter, warriors have also massed against the northern perimeter walls, but two Highland companies are steadfastly holding firm.

"They could not stand the irresistible Shock of our Men," wrote Bouquet in his dispatches, "who, rushing in among them, killed many of them & put the rest to flight." The Highlanders pursued the Indians for 2 miles while the rest of Bouquet's force moved down to Bushy Run for much needed fresh water. The casualties from two days' fighting were 50 killed, 60 wounded, and five missing, one-third of Bouquet's column. Bushy Run was a decisive action, in spite of the small numbers engaged, as it proved to be the turning point in putting down Pontiac's uprising.

Erected on the 1758 Ticonderoga battlefield in 2000 to honor the regiment, the Black Watch memorial cairn is visited annually by clansfolk whose forebears served in the Royal Highland Regiment. A portion of the memorial was built from stones sent over by clans in Scotland. (Photo by Susan Johnson McCulloch)

MUSEUMS, MEMORIALS, AND REENACTMENT

Museums that record the exploits and everyday life of the Highland regiments in North America during the Seven Years' War can be found in Canada, the United States, and the United Kingdom. In all cases, the museums and their respective websites listed in this section have exhibits and collections that highlight the equipment, weapons, and everyday life of all 18th-century soldiers, and in the case of North American historical sites, the history of French and Indian participants as well.

Most North American sites listed below are now in the process of celebrating the 250th anniversaries of the sieges and battles that were fought at their respective locations. In the year of this book's publication, 2008, Fortress Louisburg is expected to draw large numbers in June–July when it will host a huge Grand Encampment to commemorate the 1758 Siege. Likewise, Fort Ticonderoga and Fort Pitt will also host similar commemorative events, while Québec City will see a full scale reenactment of the Battle of the Plains of Abraham in 2009.

Readers are encouraged to find further details and specific timings for North American "grand encampments," reenactments, and events at the various museum websites cited below.

Canada

Fortress Louisburg, Cape Breton, Nova Scotia. http://fortress.uccb.ns.ca/
Halifax Citadel Museum, Nova Scotia.
http://parkscanada.gc.ca/lhn-nhs/ns/halifax/index_E.asp
Signal Hill, St John's, Newfoundland.
http://www.parkscanada.gc.ca/lhn-nhs/nl/signalhill/index_e.asp
Québec Fortifications & Battlefield, Québec City, Québec.
http://www.parkscanada.gc.ca/lhn-nhs/qc/fortifications/index_E.asp
Canadian War Museum, Ottawa, Ontario.
http://www.warmuseum.ca/cwm/cwme.asp
David M. Stewart Museum, Montréal. http://www.stewart-museum.org/en/default.asp

United States

Fort Ticonderoga Museum, New York State. http://www.fort-ticonderoga.org/
Fort Niagara Museum, New York State. http://www.oldfortniagara.org/
Fort Ligonier Museum, Pennsylvania. http://www.fortligonier.org/tour.htm
Bushy Run Battlefield Park, Pennsylvania. http://www.bushyrunbattlefield.com/
Fort Pitt Museum, Pennsylvania. http://www.fortpittmuseum.com/History.html
Fort de Chartres, Illinois. http://www.state.il.us/hpa/hs/DeChartres.htm

United Kingdom

The Black Watch (Royal Highland Regiment) Museum, Perth, Scotland.
http://www.theblackwatch.co.uk/museum/
National Army Museum, Chelsea, London.
http://www.national-army-museum.ac.uk/
National War Museum of Scotland (formerly the Scottish United Services Museum). http://www.nms.ac.uk/war/main.htm
Imperial War Museum, London. http://www.iwmcollections.org.uk/overview.asp

SELECT BIBLIOGRAPHY

Amherst, Jeffery, *Journal of Jeffery Amherst. Recording the Military Career of General Amherst in America from 1758 to 1763*, ed. by J. C. Webster (Toronto: 1931)

Amherst, William, *Journal of William Amherst in America 1758–1760*, ed. by J.C. Webster (Toronto: 1931)

Bouquet, Henri, *The Papers of Henri Bouquet*, ed. by S. K. Stevens *et al.*, 6 vols, (Harrisburg: 1951–54)

Brumwell, Stephen, *Redcoats: The British Soldier and the War in the Americas, 1755–1763* (Cambridge: 2002)

Doughty, A. G. & G. W. Parmalee (eds), *The Siege of Quebec and The Battle of the Plains of Abraham....*, Vol. V (Québec: 1901)

Fortescue, J. W., *A History of the British Army*, Vol. II (London: 1899–1930)

Fraser, Malcolm, "The Capture of Quebec. A Manuscript Journal Relating to the Operations Before Québec From 8th May, 1759, to 17th May, 1760. Kept by Colonel Malcolm Fraser. Then Lieutenant in the 78th Foot (Fraser's Highlanders)," *Journal of the Society for Army Historical Research [JSAHR]*, Vol. XVIII (1939) 135–68

Fyers, E. W. H., "The Loss and Recapture of St John's, Newfoundland in 1762," *JSAHR*, Vol. XI (1932) 179–215.

Guy, A. J., *Oeconomy and Discipline: Officership and Administration in the British Army 1714–1763* (Manchester: 1985)

Harper, J. R., *The Fraser Highlanders* (Montréal: 1979).

Houlding, J. A., *Fit for Service: The Training of the British Army 1715–1795* (Oxford: 1981)

Kirk[wood], Robert, *Through So Many Dangers: The Memoirs and Adventures of Robert Kirk, Late of the Royal Highland Regiment*, ed. by Ian McCulloch & Tim Todish (Fleichmanns, NY: 2004 [reprint of Limerick edition: c.1775])

Knox, John, *The Siege of Quebec and the Campaigns in North America, 1757–1760* (London: 1769)

Lloyd, E. M., "The Raising of the Highland Regiments in 1757," *English Historical Review*, Vol. XVII (1902) 466–69.

Mante, Thomas, *The History of the Late War in North America...* (London: 1772)

McCulloch, Ian Macpherson, *Sons of the Mountains: The Highland Regiments in the French & Indian War, 1756–1767* (Fleichmanns, NY: 2006).

McKellar, Patrick, *A Short Account of the Expedition Against Quebec in the Year 1759* (Quebec: 1878)

Miller, James, *Memoirs of an Invalid, U1350/Z9 & Z9A*, (Maidstone Centre for Kentish Studies: [n.d.])

"Monypenny Orderly Book", *Bulletin of the Fort Ticonderoga Museum [BFTM]*, Vol. II, 6 (July 1932) 219–51; Vol. XII, 5 (December 1969) 328–57; Vol. XII, 6 (October 1970) 434–61; Vol. XIII, 1 (December 1970) 89–116; Vol. XIII, 2 (June 1971) 151–84

Murray, James, *Journal of the Siege of Quebec from 18th September 1759 to 25th May 1760* (Toronto: 1939)

Pargellis, S. M. (ed.), *Military Affairs in North America 1758–1763: Selected Documents from the Cumberland Papers in Windsor Castle* (London & New York: 1936)

Stacey, C.P., *Quebec, 1759: The Siege and the Battle*, ed. by D.G. Graves (Toronto: [revised ed.] 2002)

Stewart of Garth, D., *Sketches of the Highlanders of Scotland* (Edinburgh: 1822)

Wallace, R. F. H., "Regimental Routine and Army Administration in North America in 1759", *JSAHR*, Vol. XXXIII (1955) 2–4.

Westbrook, Nicholas (ed.), "'Like Roaring Lions Breaking FromTheir Chains': The Highland Regiment at Ticonderoga," *BFTM*, Vol. XVI, 2 (1999) 16–91

A monument to generals Murray and Lévis and their forces that fought on April 28, 1760, outside Québec stands on the former site of Dumont's Mill, which marked the extreme left flank of the British army and was the scene of fierce hand-to-hand fighting between Highlanders and French grenadiers. Designed by the famous architect-engineer, Charles Baillairgé, it consists of a large column or pillar surmounted by the Roman goddess of war, Bellona. (Photo by author)

INDEX

Figures in **bold** refer to illustrations. Plates are shown with their location in brackets.